PEACE QUEST

JOURNEY WITH PURPOSE.

Nurturing peace within the self, relationships, society, and the planet.

WRITTEN BY KELLY GUINAN
ILLUSTRATED BY DOROTHIA ROHNER

Published in the United States by Kind Regards LLC
P.O. Box 33, Blair, NE 68008
www.celebratingpeace.com

Artwork by ~
Dorothia Rohner
Marla Blevins
Amy Calloway
Kelly Guinan
Drew Guinan
Barb Kobe

Cover layout and design by Dorothia Rohner
Layout and design by Kelly Guinan

Library of Congress Control Number: 2002090950
ISBN 0-9719279-0-1

IN APPRECIATION

To the people who have accompanied me on my journey, words cannot express my gratitude. You have influenced my life in positive ways and have encouraged me to follow my dreams and listen to my heart.

My family ~ Kristen, Ashley, Drew, Angie, and Tom

To those I have met along the way, thank you for your support and for contributing to the development of this resource in both tangible and intangible ways.

Carmen DeHart
Nori Barber
Diane & Bob Kyser
Jim Hannah
Wayne Ham
Malinda Jepsen
Melanie Blevins
Barb Kernohan
Mary Ooko
Ken Schnell
Bob Smith
Marge Nelson
Gail Mengel
Steve Veazey & Cathi Cackler-Veazey
Dave & Carolyn Brock
Carol & David Birks
Mike & Cheryl Smith
Deb Friesz
Laurie Bunten
Lynne Baller
Pat Reeves
Dorothia Rohner
Nori Barber
Barbara Kobe
Sandee Gamet
Aaron Jepsen
Brian Gibson

Diane Rockwood
Carolyn McCracken
Lori Hunzeker
Don Ivans
Judy & Scott Harrington
Bill Sample
Jean & Reed Holmes
Carolyn McCracken
Peter Judd
Barbara Higdon
Diane Mann
Patti Gubbels
Dagny Taggart
Marla Blevins
Debbie Lizer
Anne Green
Candice Brunswick
Tammie Stettler
Ronda Harvey Shaheen
Mike Friesz
Anne Romig
Violet Campbell
Amy Calloway
Charles & Alice Shakespeare
Shelly Johnson
Kim Clark
Zona Ragan

Lucy Mitchell
John & Carol White
Will & Lynne Houtchens
Ralph & Oma Rogers
Marge Nilsen
Connie Elgin
Charmaine Chvala-Smith
Karen Grinberg
Mary Jacks Dynes
Larry & Carole Anne Green
Rosie and Beaner Moore
The employees of Perfection Press
Many, many other volunteers who lead the programs and share their expertise

CONTENTS

CONTENTS

CONTENTS

JOURNEY WITH PURPOSE

I have struggled with the content of this page. There is simply no way to express the magnitude of the transformative power I have experienced as I have done my best to honor and live the principles of peace. One night as I was drifting off to sleep, I was energized by the words which to me signify the essence of a life-style of peacemaking.

> I know my purpose.
> I believe in what I'm doing.
> I am willing to pay the price.

I am awed by the realization that from this place of absolute trust and total vulnerability, anything is possible.

They are simple and profound truths which are not easy to live. The quest of peacemaking is a heartfelt yearning which provides the challenge of justice, the understanding of compassion, the awareness of abundance, and the hope for a new way of being.

This holistic approach to peacemaking engages skill building within persons, in their daily relationships, on a global community level, and in planetary care.

The soul unfolds itself, like a lotus of countless petals.
~ Kahlil Gibran

PEACE FOR ME

Peace for Me instills a sense of awareness and acceptance of the essence of personhood.

I am so incredibly grateful to know the people my children are, I cannot even begin to express the privilege it is to be their mom. I have used the four peace section headings to relate personal experiences about my children and how the skills contained within each section have helped to form and direct their lives.

As a two year old, Angie created a remarkable way of testing boundaries and processing cause and effect relationships. She created imaginary friends – Sam, Bop, and Bobby. These friends were her peers, but when they would do naughty things she would switch into a parental role and talk with them about what choice would have been better. One example was when Sam and Bop chose to leave the fenced backyard. Angie was quite upset at "their" decision and called them back into the security of her home. Through this creative expression, she was able to explore in a completely safe way, empowering herself with the ability to look at the consequences of a decision from several different dimensions. She has faced the challenges of growing up with great grace, finding her own way and developing her giftedness which she freely shares.

CATCH A DREAM

A dreamer is a visionary idealist who understands the world in an abstract way. Dreamers do not visualize in a delusional manner of negating what is; but rather in a contributory mode to nourish what can be. To dream is to accept and embrace life rather than be satisfied by it; to believe in, pursue, and further a hope-filled reality. It is noble in nature and often not practical within the boundaries of worldly considerations. To view existence in this optimistic way means the individual empowers him/herself to find a sense of personal potential. Consequently, the identity manifested provides internal strength, a sense of purpose, and an incredibly motivating force.

Dream catchers were made by Native Americans to sift out the bad dreams by catching them in the web and holding them until they would disappear with the day's first light. They allowed the good dreams to reach the sleeper by passing through the hole in the center. Children's dream catchers were made out of green, supple branches and included a feather to symbolize the breath of life.

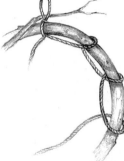

~ MATERIALS ~

- flexible stick about 24 inches long
- twine or string (3 yards)
- bead
- feather
- scissors

Bend the stick into a circle (hoop) and attach it to itself using the twine. Loop the twine up to create a hanger and tie a securing knot. Tie nine half-hitch knots spaced evenly all around the hoop. Keep the twine snug all around the hoop. (See diagram.)

To create the next inner row, tie half-hitch knots in the middle of the twine previously applied. (See diagram.) Continue in this way until the middle is reached, leaving a hole in the center of the dream catcher. Tie a couple of securing knots at the center and cut off the extra twine.

Using an additional small piece of twine, string a bead onto the twine and use it to attach the feather to the dream catcher.

Go confidently in the direction of your dreams! Live the life you've only imagined.
~ Thoreau

SHARE some of the hopes and dreams you have for your own life.
Share the dreams you have for a peaceful world.

STRONGER THAN YOU THINK

Courage is the ability to act even when faced with great fear or a sense of incompetency. There is no truth in the statement, "A courageous person is fearless." If there really was a fear-less-ness, there would be no victory because nothing would have been risked or overcome. Courage, or strength of will, exercises behavioral integrity which permits individuals to stand by their value systems in authentic ways. Courage is an internal power, which when brought to the surface, provides the ability to work for justice, sometimes alone. Great courage empowers people to do what seems impossible. It is the lifeblood of change and embraces trust at its core.

The law of gravity is an undeniable physical reality. When something is dropped, it falls to the ground.

~ MATERIALS ~

- scissors
- string
- two small spools (wooden is preferred)
- one large spool (wooden is preferred)

Construct a device as pictured. Cut the string into an 18 inch section, thread it through a middle spool, and tie each end to a small and large spool.

Hold the object by the middle spool with the smaller spool on top. The weight of the larger spool will pull the smaller spool down where it will be stopped by the middle spool. Now, ask the peacemakers to make the large spool rise without touching anything and without turning the whole thing upside down.

The task seems impossible due to the law of gravity. Demonstrate the "impossible" using the hidden energy of centripetal force by slowly swinging the top spool in a circle. As the momentum builds, the larger spool will "magically" rise.

SHARE YOUR THOUGHTS...

- Relate the force of gravity to something in life which seems impossible. What would happen if all people would look deep within themselves and draw on the strength which resides there?
- How would the world look different if everyone exercised courage for the cause of peace and justice?
- Tell about a time when you remained true to yourself by being courageous.

Courage is the greatest virtue. Without it, it is impossible to practice the other virtues consistently.
~ Maya Angelou

YOUR STORY

The way a person chooses to view the world can determine so much about the person's future. An attitude or focus which is uplifting challenges new growth and gives a sense of significance and purpose to living. Each person is given the gift of life, the personal legacy is for the individual to create. Everyone has the opportunity to meet the challenge of living the legacy of his/her **best** intentions. The individual's contribution to the lifeforce is distinct and the world is blessed by each offering.

~ MATERIALS ~

- pencils
- paper
- picture from page 6

Ask the peacemakers to look at the provided picture and to create a story about anything on the picture they see. Because of their interests and experiences, each person will naturally focus on a different aspect of the picture in telling a story. (*e.g.,* different stories may be written about the castle, or fishing, or the butterfly coming out of the cocoon, etc.)

Read the stories to each other.

Components of a good story –
- beginning
- characters
- setting
- plot (action)
- ending

SHARE YOUR THOUGHTS ...

- Why did each person focus on a particular key element for the story?
- How does including each person's story describe the picture in a more complete way?
- Why is it important to have a positive focus about life?
- What would happen if only one person's story represented the whole picture?
- Celebrate the unique view of each writer. Relate this view to the worth of each person.

TREASURES WITHIN

People who understand their intrinsic worth are secure in their sense of self. They are able to risk to learn new skills and are willing to make difficult decisions based upon their priorities and value system. They empower themselves to follow their sense of personal calling. "Begin within" is certainly an applicable phrase for the peacemaking process because this understanding of self worth allows the expression of respect, support and encouragement to others.

~ MATERIALS ~
- pencils
- copies of page 8
- shoe box
- small mirror
- wrapping paper
- tape

Give a copy of the treasure chest found on page 8 to each peacemaker. Ask the peacemakers to write down the things they consider valuable.

When all peacemakers have recorded their answers, invite them to share why these things are important and considered to be valuable. This first list may only contain physical items such as money or toys.

Connect the idea of value or worth to the intangible by asking, "What is something you can't touch that is very important to you?" After a short discussion on the merits of internal traits, ask the peacemakers to once again write on their paper what they consider to be precious or valuable – this time only writing the things they carry inside of them.

The best and most beautiful things in the world cannot be seen or even touched. They must be felt with the heart.
~ Helen Keller

Decorate a shoe box like a present. Place a mirror in the bottom of the box with a tag on the outside of the box which says, "The world's most precious gift." Direct each peacemaker to look within the box to see the gift one at a time. (The "Aha" moment is dependent upon the discovery of each person's own reflection, so ask the peacemakers not to discuss what's in the box until everyone has a chance to look.)

SHARE YOUR THOUGHTS ...

- How do you know when something is important or valuable to you?
- What is more important than things?
- What does it mean if something is called precious or valuable?
- Quietly think about the parts of yourself you treasure and what you need to do to value those parts.

BEAUTIFUL MUSIC

The joyful abandon found within toddlers' self-image as they streak the moment clothes are removed from their body is quickly replaced by extreme self-consciousness and many times self-loathing as they become inundated by society's obsession with physical appearance. Rather than honoring the different body types, an unobtainable, often unhealthy model is held up as the ideal. Females are most susceptible to the detrimental effects often resulting in a feeling of "not good enough," depression, eating disorders, and extremely poor choices in other areas of life because she sees herself as fundamentally flawed. The answer of course is to place the focus on healthy living which values the self in a holistic way, seeing the physique as simply one part of a wonderfully made creature. The individuality expressed through the different sizes, shapes, colors, appearance, and abilities of the physical form should be celebrated! The design and miraculous nature of each and every person needs to be exalted.

~MATERIALS ~
- paper
- glue
- scissors
- copies of page 10

The peacemakers will take the "Beautiful Music" pages and create a song by arranging the pictures in any way they choose. The pictures of different body parts making sound are cut apart and glued on a piece of paper.

After the pictures are glued in place, follow the directions (clap, foot stomp, whistle, snap, tongue cluck) and perform your unique song for the other peacemakers. Try performing each person's original song together.

SHARE in a discussion relating each unique song and the preciousness of each life. Spend some time emphasizing the importance of valuing all parts of the personhood and not allowing others to make us feel worthless.

10

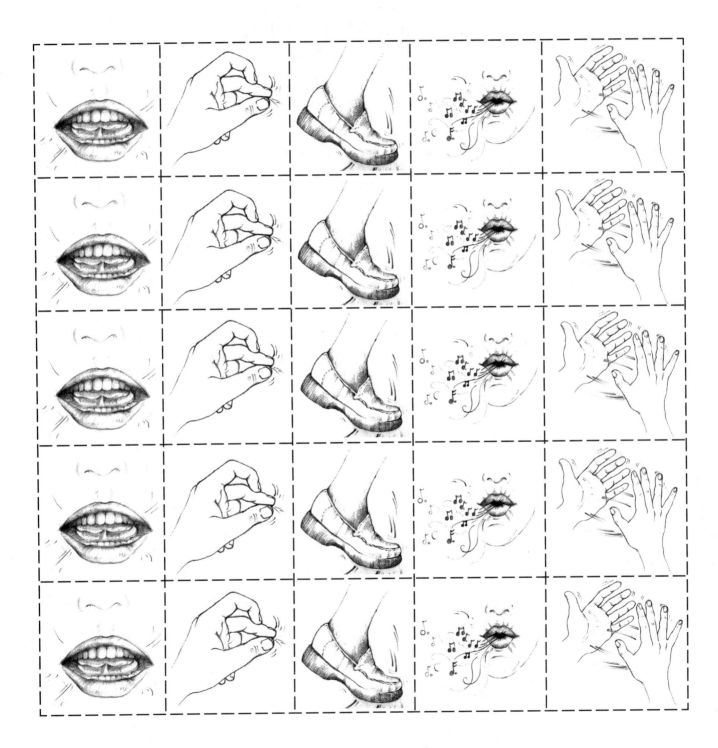

HARMONY

Yoga is an ancient discipline, a synthesis of all parts of the being. In recent years many people have chosen to practice the poses for a variety of different reasons ranging from simple relaxation to exercise. The purposeful breathing is helpful in centering and directing the mind into a receptive mode, relieving stress by calming the noise of the outside world and focusing emotional energy. The steady body postures strengthen the muscles, increase flexibility, and improve circulation. The balance of the poses and counterposes offer nourishment and create harmony and well-being.

~ MATERIALS ~
- instant camera
- permanent markers
- copies of page 12

Give the peacemakers the illustrations so they can practice the positions. The poses are more difficult than they appear and take strength and concentration. Encourage the peacemakers to try to do them properly and to relax into the pose. Use an instant camera and take a picture of the peacemakers when they are comfortable in the positions.

Discuss how the constellations were named because people looked at groupings of stars and with the use of their imagination, created shapes and symbols representing their folklore and myths.

Using the marker and the developed instant picture, imagine what form could be constructed from the pose and draw the image outline on the picture. (The examples on the illustrations are simply that, examples. Other possibilities should be encouraged.)

SHARE together times you have tried something new and had fun doing it.
Why is it important to remember to take care of our bodies, minds, and emotions?

ONE WHOLE PERSON

Touch has been used for centuries as a healing art. It is the most highly developed sense we are born with and the last sense that leaves the body. Doctors are aware that one of the strongest healing agents with premature infants involves the merging of modern technology with the simple act of being held. Some people have practiced the art of rubbing the feet in certain places because they believe this touch can balance and soothe the entire body. The reflex points and the organs they are believed to refresh, revitalize, and assist in a general way are identified in the chart with this lesson.

The sense of smell is also used in holistic ways. Recently, students have even been encouraged to study with a particular scent and then to reintroduce that scent into their environment at test time as a way of stimulating memory. Aromatherapy is a type of herbology and, as such, studies the effects of essential oils and scents on the body. Just as drinking a tea made of chamomile, ginger, and spearmint can reduce stress and calm the body, smelling certain scents can influence one's mood and other personal characteristics. Many researchers believe that essential oils applied to the body can stimulate the immune system to prevent and fight disease. Other people use them simply because they are a delight to the senses.

~ MATERIALS ~
- scented lotion or ingredients to make your own rub
- water
- copies of page 14

SERENITY RUB -
Use caution when creating your own rub, essential oils are VERY concentrated and at full strength can be highly irritating to the skin.

5 drops lavendar oil
1 drop chamomile oil
1 drop bergamot oil

Mix together in a lotion. Or to create an exfoliating scrub, mix together in 1 Tbsp. of coarse salt (*e.g.*, Epsom or Kosher salt).

Smell is a potent wizard that transports you across thousands of miles and all the years you have lived.
~ Helen Keller

Using the diagram of the feet and the scented lotion, give yourself a foot massage or take turns giving each other massages.

SHARE ideas about how the body is made up of parts which work together as a whole. In other words, talk about the cause and effect relationship behaviors have on the entire body – not just on one part. What happens when a person doesn't get enough sleep, smokes cigarettes, eats too much candy, etc? List some positive behaviors people can do to help their bodies perform at their best.

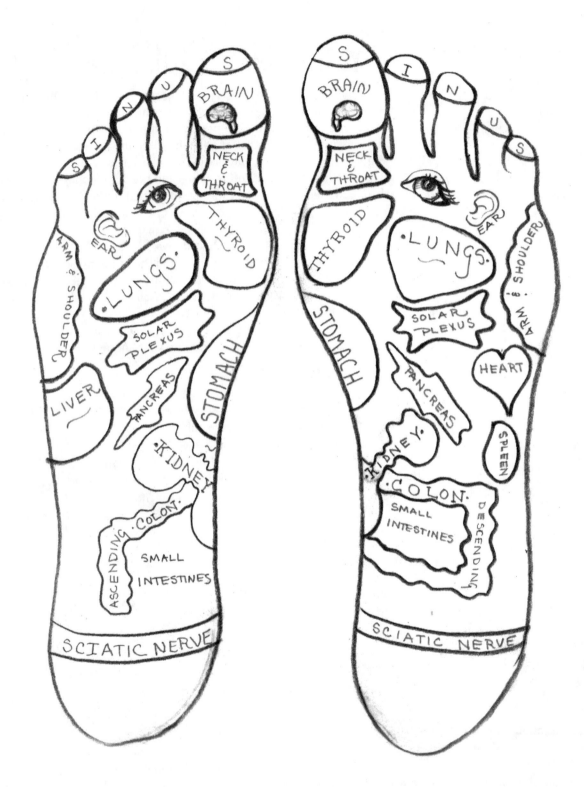

IN MY "RIGHT" MIND

Research indicates one of the reasons people process life differently is found within the duality of the brain. Theories suggest the right and left hemispheres of the brain are complementary but specialized in their function, each side responsible for certain characteristics and methods. The modes of thinking associated with left brained dominance are: analytical, logical, sequential, objective, verbal, and a pattern user, while those attributed to the right brain are intuitive, relational, creative, mystical, divergent, and a pattern seeker. Realistically, the way a person learns or knows something is an integration of a cohesive whole, but an awareness in the primary and preferred manner an individual uses to regard the world is helpful for self-knowledge and in creating understanding between people.

~ MATERIALS ~
- crayons
- scissors
- copies of page 16

Advance preparation – Prior to the activity, make two copies of the following page. Color the words any color except for the color the letters spell. For example, the word "blue" can be colored red, the word "yellow" can be colored black, etc. Cut the color words apart on the lines indicated and set them in a pile. With the second page you have copied, color the area around the word in a color that does not correspond to the word. This creates a negative image effect. For example, the word "blue" will remain white, but the word's outer block will be red. Cut these words apart and set them in a second pile.

Use the first pile as flash cards and go through each card with every peacemaker. Show each card quickly as the peacemakers say each color out loud. (Your group will be dividing itself into those who think predominantly with the right hemisphere of their brains and those who think with their left. The people who say the color which is written on the card are left brained, the people who say the color of the word are right brained.)

Repeat the experiment using the negative image or second set of cards. (In this case, the outcome is reversed as the left brained people see the color while the right brained people read the white words.)

SHARE in a discussion of how differences in how people actually see the world create problems, and in how this difference is helpful. Emphasize there is no "right" way of perceiving the world, simply different ways.

MAKE IT ACROSS

The vast mental resources that lie within the brain are virtually untapped. Learning is a lifelong process which opens the mind to new understanding while increasing the skill base of the individual. The mind, however, needs to be stretched and stimulated in order for the brain cells and synapses to remain healthy and active.

~ MATERIALS ~
• toothpicks
• pencils
• copies of page 18

Stretch your "mental muscles" by finding the best solution to the following problems –

Using 6 toothpicks, see how many triangles can be made with one design. (We think the highest answer is 16.)

The child must transport the dog, the cat, and the cat food in as few trips as possible to the other shore. The problem is, the child cannot carry more than one item in the boat at the same time. The cat and dog cannot be left alone or they will fight. The cat and cat food can't be left alone together or the cat will eat all the food and get sick.

1. The child takes the cat in the boat to the other side and returns.

2. The child takes the cat food to the other side and returns with the cat in the boat.

3. The child leaves the cat on the close shore and takes the dog to the other side in the boat and returns.

4. The child takes the cat to the other side.

There is nothing like returning to a place that remains unchanged to find the ways in which you yourself have altered.
~ Nelson Mandela

SHARE YOUR THOUGHTS ...

• How do you solve problems?
• Why is it important to study and learn new things?

MAKE IT ACROSS

TALKING TO MYSELF

Self confidence develops, in part, as a result of accepting a realistic, honest, yet positive awareness of both strengths and weaknesses. The tone of a person's internal dialog can maximize the chance for success or set up failure even before an effort has been made. There is a mind - body connection which actually creates the positive energy to make amazing impracticalities possible. The means is to simply believe in internal convictions, follow the heart, and create a personal destiny.

~ MATERIALS ~
- scissors
- copy of this page

Cut apart the statement cards. Pick a card and read it aloud. Ask the peacemakers to give a "thumbs up" sign if the statement reflects a positive self-image or a "thumbs down" if the statement shows a negative self-image. Ask the peacemakers to change the negative statements into positive statements. Discuss how positive and negative self talk affects our feelings and behaviors.

"It's hard, but I think I can do it."

"I want to try lots of things."

"I can't do it, I'm just not smart."

"They would never vote for me."

"I think I have a funny sense of humor."

"I think I look stupid."

"Nothing I try ever turns out, I'm going to just stop trying."

"I hate being so dumb."

"I could never have a job like that, I'm just not good enough."

"I might not win, but it will be fun to try."

"I don't know why she doesn't like me, I think I'm really nice."

"I really worked hard and did my best, I feel proud."

SHARE YOUR THOUGHTS ....

- Give some examples of the kinds of things you say to yourself everyday. Are most of these statements "thumbs up" statements or "thumbs down" statements? How do positive statements help you to be your best and try new things?
- How do you think life would be different if you looked in the mirror every day and said, "I am special. I am loved. Today I will try my best, and that's enough."? Try this every day for two weeks.

THE FULLS

Feelings are incredibly motivating, provide a sense of meaning to relationships, and determine the difference between mere existence and the passion of the human experience. Feelings simply are, without value judgement. In practice, however, they are assigned the stigma of being either "good" or "bad." To repeat, feelings simply are, they are not good or bad. Any feeling is fine. It is the expression of the feeling which can have positive or negative effects. To deny what is determined as a "negative" feeling only suppresses it rather than allows a normal and healthy processing of the emotion. The ability to embrace the emotion and work through it toward a resolution provides closure and the prospect of wellness.

~ MATERIALS ~

- crayons
- scissors
- glue
- copies of pages 22-24

Sit together on a rug on the floor and let the peacemakers examine and hold the "Fulls." Ask the peacemakers what they think the Fulls might be named, giving them the clue that their faces and colors express their names. Identify all the Fulls and each feeling in this way. Numbfull is tough for people to figure out so you may have to name it and tell the peacemakers that it is so confused it doesn't know how it feels. It has blocked out its feelings and gone numb.

Use the following scenario as a guide. As you begin storytelling in your own words, gather each Full at the appropriate moment and hold it in your hands so everyone can see when its part of the story unfolds.

Begin by asking the peacemakers if there was ever a time when they went somewhere and didn't know anyone at all. Perhaps it was the first day of school. Ask them how they felt in that moment of total isolation. When someone says they were afraid, ask for "Fearfull" and relate that, yes, it is scary. In fact too scary, so you decided to stuff that feeling down deep where no one can see it. (Place Fearfull inside of Numbfull's front pouch.)

Ask the peacemakers if you really took care of the fear or if you simply hid it away. Because that emotion hasn't truly been dealt with, the situation escalates and the person begins to feel something else. (Facial expression like you're going to cry is nice here.) A peacemaker will say "Tearfull" when asked how the person is feeling now. Take Tearfull into your hands. Share that the person started off only afraid, then didn't want all the strangers to see him/her cry. They've already stuffed down one feeling rather than take care of it, so what will they decide to do with this emotion? (Use body language to indicate stuffing it in Numbful too.) Point out that a pattern has developed.

Go on with the story. The person has all of this going on and they get into the classroom and they start acting (point to Sillyfull and bring it up into your hands) silly. Describe "class clown" behavior – making faces, tapping someone on the shoulder, talking when they are not supposed to. This person is stuck in silly. The peacemakers can easily identify this characteristic. In the discussion, ask if they ever thought maybe the person who was acting so goofy was doing so because they didn't want people to know they were hurt or scared.

Bring up how Numbfull might be feeling now – not only confused, scared, and sad, but now it has a tummy ache from stuffing the emotions.

As the storytelling goes on, the person who is stuck in Sillyfull gets sent to the principal's office and now must feel what? (Stuff Sillyfull inside Numbfull.) When "Awfull" is identified, hold it up and then ask what the pattern says you're going to do (stuff it into Numbfull too).

Now, almost at the principal's door and what is the feeling? "Ragefull!" Ask who you are mad at, is it the teacher's fault, the person who laughed at your joke, or you? (The individual is responsible, and the anger is basically toward the whole world as well as themselves.)

When the person is at this point with all this built up emotion, the only thing that can happen is an explosion. (Pull the Fulls out of Numbfull one at a time tossing them randomly around naming everything the person is mad about as the Fulls are tossed in the air.) Point out that the chaos happened all because someone was scared and didn't know what to do.

Now take some time to process what a positive way of dealing with the feelings could have been. Embrace Powerfull and Peacefull at this point and tell the peacemakers that they only work when they hold hands with someone else. If Fearfull holds Powerfull's hands, it has the strength to express the emotion in a positive way (list ideas) and when that happens, Peacefull joins hands on the other side of Fearfull. Continue the discussion on powerful and peaceful ways of expressing each of the emotions represented by the Fulls.

Share how the only healthy, happy way to live is if we all choose to hold hands. Have the peacemakers hold hands with each other and with the Fulls in a circle. Dance around the circle singing, "I Want to be a Peacemaker," found on page 130.

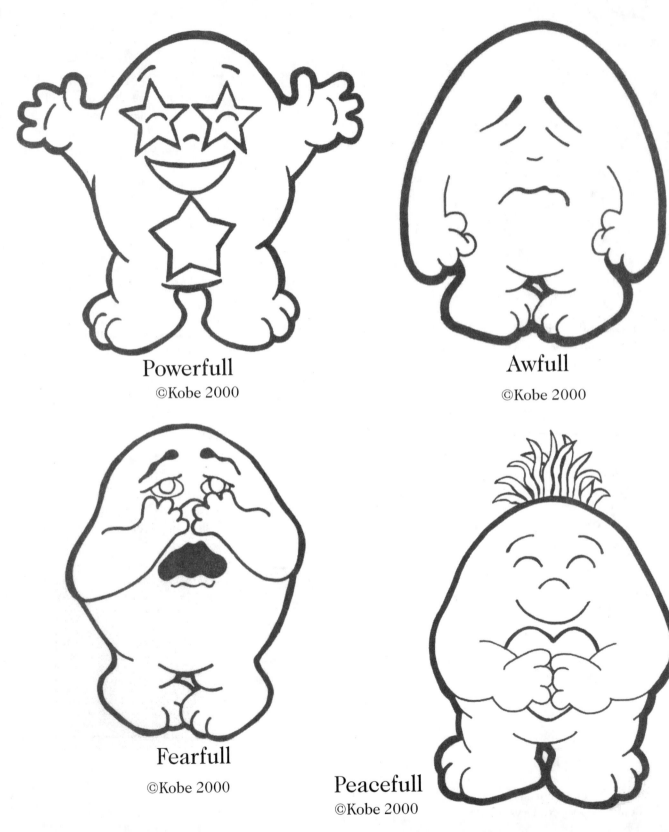

Powerfull

©Kobe 2000

Awfull

©Kobe 2000

Fearfull

©Kobe 2000

Peacefull

©Kobe 2000

Glue pocket on Numbfull's tummy leaving top open

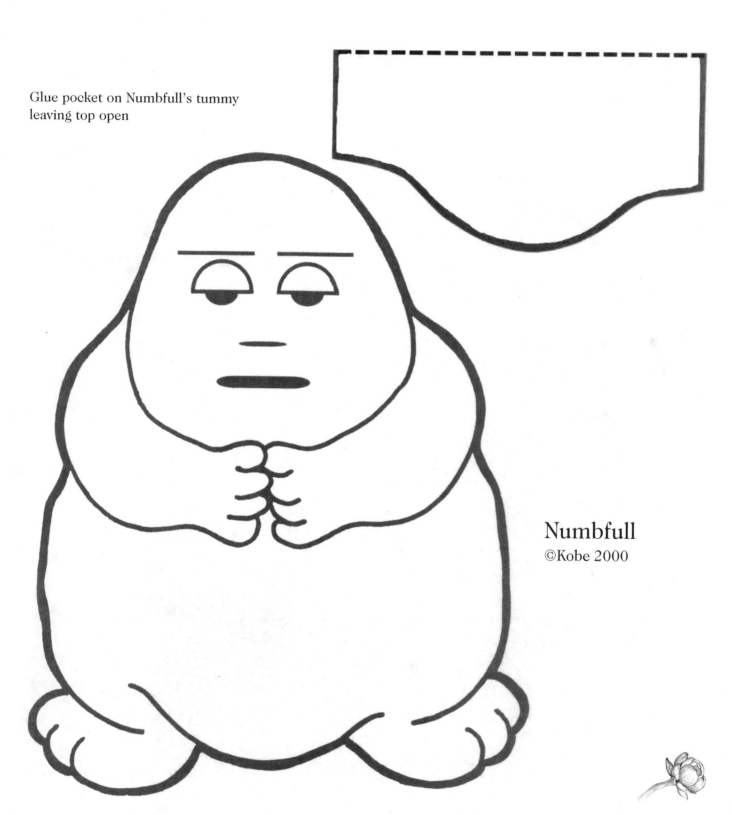

Numbfull
©Kobe 2000

24

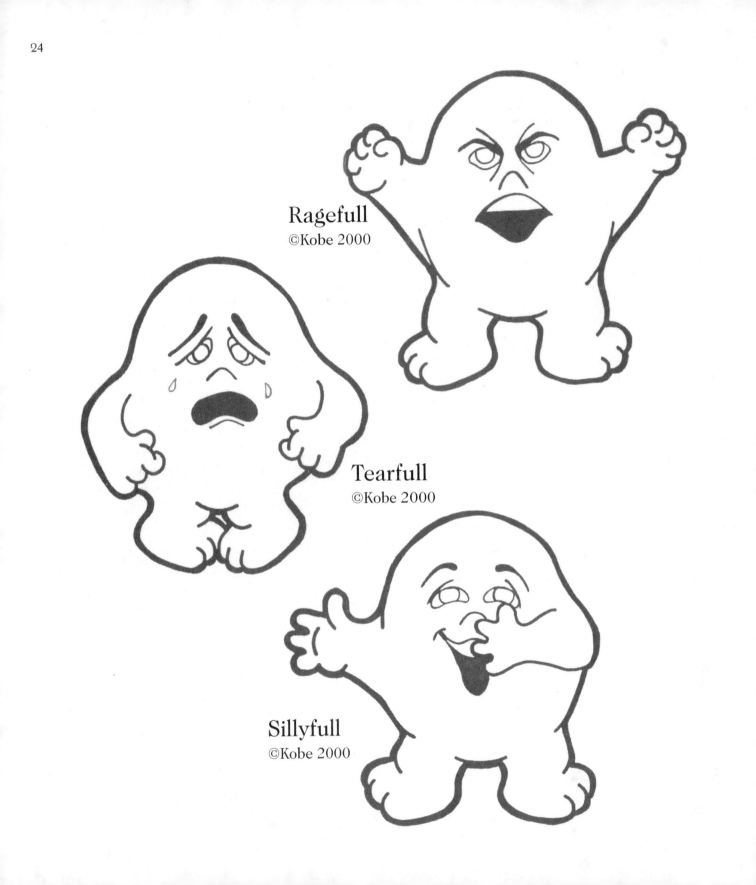

Ragefull
©Kobe 2000

Tearfull
©Kobe 2000

Sillyfull
©Kobe 2000

FEELINGS BINGO

An element of personal peace begins with the ability to recognize and identify emotions. Feelings are an important expression of personhood. They have a powerful influence on thoughts and actions. Identifying and understanding true feeling is the first step to choosing appropriate responses to those feelings.

Photocopy enough of pages 26 & 27 for each peacemaker plus one. Create a grab bag to hold "Feelings cards" by cutting apart one sheet of the "Feelings faces" and placing the pieces in the paper sack. Create individual Bingo cards by cutting "Feelings faces" pages apart and gluing the faces onto the "Feelings Bingo" cards in a variety of arrangements, making a unique card for each peacemaker.

One person will draw "Feelings faces" out of the grab bag, call out the feeling and show the card to the group. Each person who has a match to the feeling face on his/her card will mark it using a gumdrop. Four in a row (across, down, or diagonally) creates a Bingo. The peacemakers getting "Bingo" act out the feeling they Bingoed with. In order for everyone to have a chance to win, only the peacemaker with the Bingo will clear his/her card, then play continues on. (The person with the Bingo still continues to play but the odds of winning again are greatly reduced.)

~ MATERIALS ~
- copies of pages 26 & 27
- gumdrops
- glue
- scissors
- paper sack

SHARE in a discussion of healthy feeling expression. List productive ways of directing emotions – exercise, reading a book, writing in a journal, talking to someone, playing a musical instrument, centering, etc. Remember that no healthy expression involves harm coming to the self, others, or belongings.

26

FEELINGS FACES

ANGRY

DISAPPOINTED

SCARED

JOYFUL

DELIGHTED

NERVOUS

PEACEFUL

MIXED-UP

EXCITED

UPSET

SAD

HAPPY

DREAMY

JEALOUS

SICK

SLEEPY

FEELINGS BINGO
CARDS

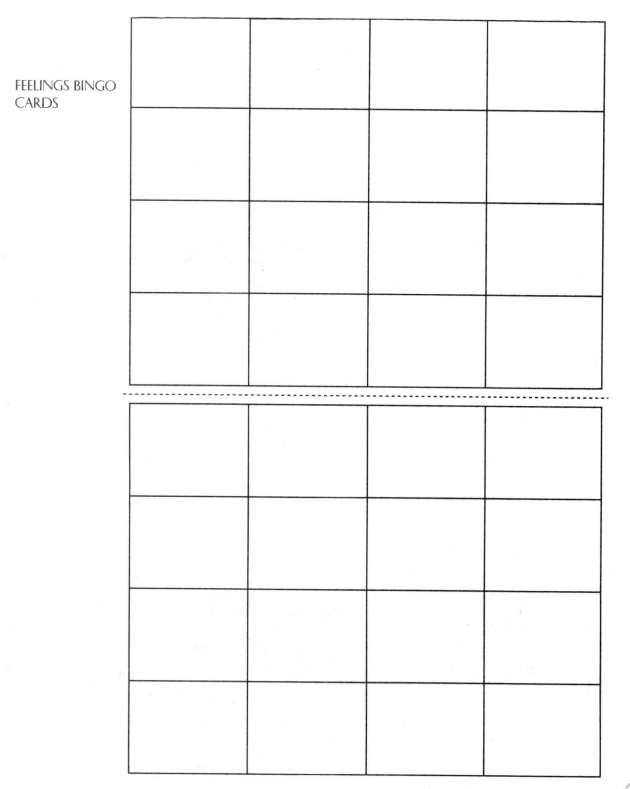

UNDER THE MASK

The quest to find the authentic self carries with it the responsibility to accept and embrace the whole person. People create masks to camouflage real thoughts and feelings, to project the image of themselves they want others to know. The masks are an illusion which can and do actually take the place of the genuine person. They are a defense device, a barrier, which prevents others from in fact knowing the true individual.

Societal roles are used as excuses to wear different masks in order to interact with others. People actually convince themselves the masks are in place to help other people. In reality, they are in place as much or more for the individual as they are for the outside world. Masks are denial mechanisms so the person doesn't ever have to fully accept the truth of who they are. There is a payoff when someone chooses to wear a mask. The journey of self-discovery and knowledge is the most arduous trek a person can make. Not only is there the uncovering of the complexities of the human condition, but it forces the individual to face their shadow side as well as confront his/her own greatness and to take full responsibility for his/her life path.

Internal power is only actualized through the exercise of embracing the authentic self and allowing vulnerability. It is only when a person is truly at ease with her/himself and transparent to others that the personal and interpersonal peace process is fully empowered.

~ MATERIALS ~
- paper
- popsicle sticks
- glue
- scissors
- crayons or markers
- yarn

Discuss with the peacemakers the concept of wearing masks to hide thoughts and feelings. Use common, everyday examples such as not wanting to let someone see you cry for fear of being made fun of as a reason to "put on a happy face." Other ideas can come from the roles they are aware of and the masks created from expectations of the role. Instruct the peacemakers to make their own masks. Role play situations where they express themselves from their real perspective, and then from the perspective the mask "demands."

SHARE with each other ways each person can be more genuine in who they really are, as well as ways each person can make it safer for others to express their true self.

A SIGN OF HOW I FEEL

Experiences of life evoke many different feelings. Sometimes these feelings are clear and easy to label, other times they are hard to identify. There are even times when contradictory emotions are felt simultaneously. An important first step in expressing emotion, is to identify what it is so appropriate responses can be chosen.

~ MATERIALS ~
• copy of this page

Learning sign language for emotions and feelings is a fun way for peacemakers to recognize and name their feelings. Share some or all of the signs below with the peacemakers. Have them share their feelings with each other using these signs.

SAD	LOVE	ANGER	LONELY
HAPPY	SHY	HATE	HURT
SORRY	PROUD	CONTENT	FEAR

Share in discussion times when each peacemaker has felt the different emotions shown here. Then take the time for another fun activity – relate colors with feelings in a personal way. "Yellow reminds me of feeling excited when I went to the beach this summer and the sun was big and bright."

FACING THE FEAR MONSTERS

All feelings are a natural part of the human experience. Fear is one of the feelings which are judged as negative and something to be avoided. (Emotions are not positive or negative.) It accompanies experiences, or the anticipation of experiences, which are perceived to be dangerous or unfamiliar. Fear is a natural reaction. It is a safety reflex, adrenaline surges with instinctual fight or flight response. Fear can also become unrealistic though and paralyze the growth of a person by preventing him/her from participating fully in life and risking failure.

~ MATERIALS ~
- crayons
- copies of page 31

Photo copy "Fear Monster" activity page for each peacemaker. Ask them to write some of the things that make them afraid in the monster's spots. Change the scary monster into a friendly monster by giving it a big smile and coloring it bright, exciting colors.

We gain strength, courage, and confidence by each experience in which we really stop to look fear in the face...we must do that which we think we cannot.
~ Eleanor Roosevelt

SHARE YOUR THOUGHTS ....

- List ways your fears can be used to help you stay safe.
- What is the difference in realistic and unrealistic fears?
- What can you do to overcome unrealistic fears?

TAKING MY FEELINGS TEMPER-ATURE

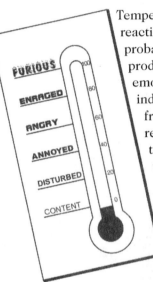

Temper is a disposition, a state of mind. It is usually associated with an angry outburst in reaction to a stimulus. The more emotional intensity behind a circumstance, the higher probability of a harmful or destructive response. The key to directing emotion into productive means is in taking the power back into the cognitive side and not letting the emotion control the person. Changing the word emphasis of the internal dialog allows the individual to determine his/her response. For instance, instead of remaining in the frustration of "that" makes me so mad, rephrasing offers the opportunity to take responsibility for what the individual is feeling, thinking, and ultimately doing – I choose to be mad when "that" happens. The power this simple attitudinal change makes within the individual eases the level of intensity allowing the circumstance to become more manageable.

~ MATERIALS ~

- crayon
- copies of page 33

Discuss with the peacemakers how feelings heighten when we find ourselves in frustrating or difficult situations. Define and discuss "temper." Clarify the difference between feelings and actions, such as: "I feel annoyed" vs. "I feel like slapping him." Discuss how actions and responses tend to change with the intensity of a situation. It is much easier to direct our responses to a situation when we are a little disturbed or annoyed than it is when we are enraged or furious. When we identify early that our "temper-ature" is rising, we are better able to take safe and appropriate actions.

Pass out the copies of page 33. Read aloud the situations, ask the peacemakers to color the accompanying thermometers showing how they would feel in each situation. Discuss the possible healthy, peaceful responses to each situation.

SHARE YOUR THOUGHTS...

- Did everyone feel the same about each situation? Explain.
- Why did some of the situations raise your temper-ature more than others?
- Did your possible responses tend to change the angrier you were? Give an example.
- What are some of the rules for expressing anger in positive and healthy ways?

33

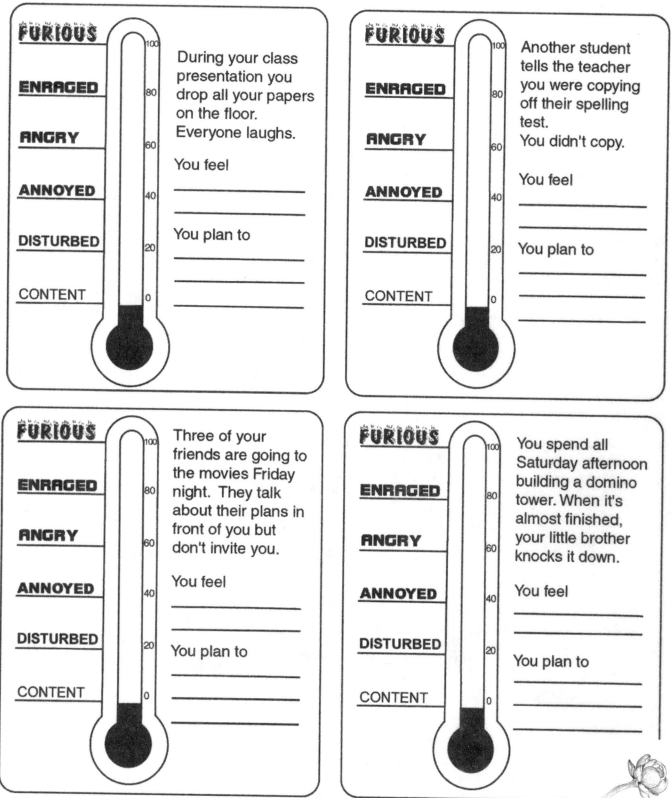

FURIOUS

ENRAGED — 80

ANGRY — 60

ANNOYED — 40

DISTURBED — 20

CONTENT — 0

During your class presentation you drop all your papers on the floor. Everyone laughs.

You feel
_____
_____

You plan to
_____
_____
_____

FURIOUS

ENRAGED — 80

ANGRY — 60

ANNOYED — 40

DISTURBED — 20

CONTENT — 0

Another student tells the teacher you were copying off their spelling test.
You didn't copy.

You feel
_____
_____

You plan to
_____
_____
_____

FURIOUS

ENRAGED — 80

ANGRY — 60

ANNOYED — 40

DISTURBED — 20

CONTENT — 0

Three of your friends are going to the movies Friday night. They talk about their plans in front of you but don't invite you.

You feel
_____
_____

You plan to
_____
_____
_____

FURIOUS

ENRAGED — 80

ANGRY — 60

ANNOYED — 40

DISTURBED — 20

CONTENT — 0

You spend all Saturday afternoon building a domino tower. When it's almost finished, your little brother knocks it down.

You feel
_____
_____

You plan to
_____
_____
_____

LEAVE YOUR WORRIES

Occasional anxious moments and concerns are part of the daily backdrop of life. It is when these characteristics take on more importance than they merit and when they become the crux of life that they become disruptive to a holistic life-style. Constant worrying indicates the person is not living in the moment but rather is preoccupied with what might be in the future. This time spent in anxiety about things which can't be controlled and probably won't even materialize robs the person of the present.

In different cultures, an object is sometimes used to symbolize the desire to release the burden of worry. At times, it is a small "worry rock" carried in a pocket and rubbed when the holder feels agitated. At other times, worry dolls are made to "carry" the owner's burdens for them.

~ MATERIALS ~

- wooden clothespins with round head
- small wooden sticks
- wood glue
- markers
- craft glue
- yarn
- tea or coffee

The wooden clothespin will be the head, torso, and legs of the worry doll. To create different skin tones, soak the clothes pins and sticks for various lengths of time in very strong tea or coffee. Using wood glue, dry clothespins and sticks, glue the sticks on to the clothespin to create "arms."

When the doll form has dried, anchor a section of brightly colored yarn to the "body" with craft glue and begin wrapping the yarn around the midsection, down and up each "leg," and then back up the midsection ending in the "armpit" area, anchoring it again with craft glue. At the back of the "neck," anchor another piece of yarn with the craft glue, tucking the end slightly lower. Then begin wrapping the "neck, shoulders, and arms." When the sleeves have been completed, loop through the last few rounds and then continue wrapping onto the midsection as shown. Tuck the yarn end into the upper midsection to hide it and then secure the end with craft glue. Use the markers to draw the face and hair.

Worry does not empty tomorrow of sorrow – it
empties today of strength.
~ Corrie ten Boom

SHARE together concerns and what types of action plans can be implemented to lessen the concerns. Identify the kinds of troubles which the peacemakers have no control over and which simply serve to cause fear, suspicion, and distress. Talk about the kinds of coping skills which can be used to deal with these types of worries.

I'M STUCK

At times, people can become stranded within an emotion. When this happens, frustration compounds the situation and the person feels trapped and unable to process through the feeling into the next stage. Holding on to offense, pain, anger, or even silliness prevents growth and the ability to try new things. During these times, people may simply have to "act themselves into a new way of thinking," beginning the behavior which will offer the release, trusting that the feelings will then follow the behavior.

~MATERIALS ~
- cornstarch
- measuring cup
- water
- bowl
- food coloring
- spoon

In a bowl, mix together the cornstarch and water at a ratio of 2 to 1, *e.g.,* 1 cup cornstarch, 1/2 cup water. Three drops of food coloring may be added if desired. The mixture will be somewhat thick and gooey. It's now ready to squish, drip, and play with. For a more fluid substance, add more water.

When having a smackerel of something with
a friend, don't eat so much that you get
stuck in the doorway trying to get out.
~ "Pooh," A.A. Milne

SHARE YOUR THOUGHTS....

Imagine you had your hands absolutely full of garbage that you refused to take to the trash can and someone came up and offered you a beautiful present. You wouldn't be able to receive the gift until you put the garbage in its place. That's what it is like when we hold on to old grudges. How can you release resentment or feelings which are hurtful?

Relate how a "class clown" is someone who gets stuck in being silly. The person's whole identity is trapped in acting goofy and being disruptive. How easy is it for people to really know this person? How can this person begin to show other parts of her/himself?

LETTING GO

Detachment is a practice which releases the pain or hurt of a situation and allows the individual to continue on with life. It is different from denial which is an avoidance mechanism. It acknowledges reality and then disengages from it to stop the drain of essential energy.

Just as in juggling, the key to detachment is in the letting go. A disciplined practice allows each art form to become more natural and usable.

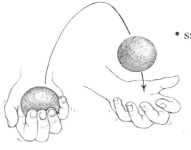

~ MATERIALS ~
• small balls or make your own bean bags

Begin by practicing with one ball. Hold the ball at waist level and throw it in an arch from one hand to the other. The top of the arch should be at about eye level.

Once competency has been reached with one ball, add a second ball. The process is the same. Throw the first ball with the left hand to catch it in the right hand. When this ball reaches the highest point in its arch, throw the second ball from the right hand to the awaiting left hand. The balls change hands in opposite arches, each leaving its base when the other is at the top of its arch. Remember to make the arch tall enough to be at about eye level.

Just as the first ball cannot be easily caught until the hand has released the second ball, people cannot receive new things until they let go of the things that are no longer important.

SHARE YOUR THOUGHTS...

• Explain what you are thinking and feeling as you are trying to learn how to juggle. ("Frustrated" is a common answer.) What do you want to do with this feeling?
• How can hanging on to resentments or other emotions keep you from growing as a person and from welcoming new ideas or people?

SUNNYSIDE UP

Humor can be a wonderful tool to help with life's ups and downs. It can also be unintentionally hurtful when used in the wrong way. When humor is used as a method of dealing with problems, special care and heightened sensitivity to the feelings of others should always be exercised. Always direct the energy to see the humor in the situation, but never use it as a way to diminish another. Sarcasm is never a healthy expression of humor.

Being able to see the silliness in something can relieve the stress so wiser decisions can be made. Laughter releases endorphins, chemicals in the brain, which actually make people feel happier and more hopeful.

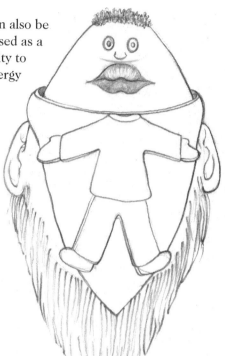

~ MATERIALS ~
- bandanna
- felt
- scissors
- glue
- washable markers
- pencils
- copies of page 38

Use the felt to create little clothes as shown in the picture. Glue the outfit to the bandanna. Take turns hanging upside down (perhaps over the edge of a couch) and place the bandanna loosely on the face as shown. Use the markers to draw a face on the chin and perhaps use more felt to create long hair. Sing a song or talk and it will appear to onlookers as if the little person is talking but with a really silly result.

Instruct the peacemakers to get into small groups to fill out "Silly Story" on page 38. One peacemaker acts as the scribe, the others provide the words without seeing their placement until the story is composed. Share the story with each other.

SHARE YOUR THOUGHTS ...

- Tell about a time when you and your family or friends laughed together.
- Give an example of how to use humor in a tense situation.

What soap is to the body, laughter is to the soul.
~ Yiddish proverb

SILLY STORY

DEFINITIONS -
NOUN ~ person, place, or thing
ADJECTIVE ~ word which describes a noun
VERB ~ action word
ADVERB ~ word which describes a verb

EXAMPLES-
house; dog
large; old
run; skip
quickly; quietly

Without letting them see the story, have the other peacemakers provide the words to fill in the blanks. Write down their responses, then read the story to each other.

Under the sea there lived a great _____. It had three _____ eyes,
NOUN   ADJECTIVE

and a large_____. It spent its day _____ing from place to place,
NOUN   VERB

looking for _____. Not knowing where to go next, it _____ sat and
PLURAL NOUN   ADVERB

thought about a_____. Then, a _____, _____ _____
NOUN   ADJECTIVE   ADJECTIVE   NOUN

came near and asked if they could be friends. The two new friends _____ed away
VERB

_____.
ADVERB

HAPPY PLACE

The benefits of the ability to simply "enjoy your bliss" cannot be overstated. The capacity to remain centered when circumstances demand turmoil helps the mind to make wiser decisions, allows the body to experience less distress, and empowers the spirit to flourish and to produce new understandings. This intuitive "place," or state of consciousness, is known as serenity and is characterized by a sense of well-being, mindfulness, discernment, and passive awareness. It goes beyond coping; it is a liberating and transforming internal power the essence of which is inner peace.

Elusive to many, this blissful state of being is often demonstrated by very young children because of their innate ability to stay focused on the present moment. Reclaiming this art and improving self-care is possible through many different techniques. The method this lesson focuses on is the potential of the imagination.

*All the works of man have their origin
in creative fantasy. What right have
we then to depreciate imagination?*
~ Carl Jung

Imagination uses the energy of the creative mind to confront and to process reality in a way that can transcend circumstances. The mental images produced by the imagination may incorporate memories of the past, images within present existence, and understandings of things to come.

~ MATERIALS ~
- crayons or colored pencils
- copies of page 40

Give the peacemakers crayons or colored pencils and a copy of page 40. As they color the picture, talk about times when they have been happy. Discuss how they think the child in the picture is feeling and what the child is thinking. Discover some of the hidden details in the picture such as the hawk circling high overhead as a symbol of protection. When the pictures are completed, invite the peacemakers to relax, to close their eyes, and to imagine themselves as the child in the picture. **Slowly** guide them with your soothing, kind voice as they imagine themselves in this happy place:

Relax your body. Close your eyes. Relax. Breathe slowly, thinking only of your breath going in and out of your body. Breathe in slowly - - one, two, three, four and out - - one, two, three, four. (Repeat these breathing instructions two more times.) Imagine yourself lying on the soft grass without a care in the world. You have just finished reading a really good story, have no worries, and are in no hurry. The sun is shining and warming your skin. The water feels calm and cool when you dip your toe into it. There is a bird singing a song just for you! Listen closely. You can even hear the fish blowing bubbles in the water to join the bird in the song. A dragonfly begins to dance to the music just above your head as you begin to hear the whisper of the wings of the butterfly gently gliding in the sky. Take a deep breath and smell the sweet scent of the flowers drifting over your body. All of nature is surrounding you in a hug. You feel the soft brush of fur on your face and realize a bunny has just kissed your cheek. There is nothing to fear. You are completely warm and safe. You begin to think of a happy memory or dream of something happy that can happen in the future. The sun is warm and wonderful on your skin. Your breathing is slow and gentle.   Just imagine.... (Allow the peacemakers personal quiet time now with their thoughts.)

SHARE, as individuals choose to, what their "Happy Place" within their own imaginations looks like. Offer times when using the imagination to create in this way is especially helpful. Consider the benefits of all people carrying a happy place within their hearts.

HAPPY PLACE

If you want to be happy, be.
~Leo Tolstoy

WALKING YOUR WAY TO PEACE

Quieting the mind relaxes the body and develops the skills for listening to the deepest expression of awareness. This calming helps individuals divest themselves from the intensity of the moment, allowing for time to make wiser and more appropriate decisions. The physiological benefits of meditation are well documented as it lowers blood pressure and pulse rate and also acts as a balm for many other bodily responses caused by distress.

The ancient custom of labyrinth walking, done in a quiet, contemplative way, is said to foster tranquility and to center a person physically, intellectually, emotionally, and spiritually. A labyrinth is a type of mandala and, as such, symbolizes through the concentric rings positioned around a center, the interconnectedness of the outer life with the inward personal journey. Labyrinths connect deep within the human psyche as they were developed separately all over the globe by many different cultures for similar expressions. They are said to represent wholeness and to signify the twists and turns of the life path.

The labyrinth is made up of two lines. One line is shown here in gray, the other in black. (The color difference is utilized for ease in construction and not desirable on the actual labyrinth.)

Create your own labyrinth by starting with the inner gray circle and by working your way out. Then, add the black circles in and around the gray.

This labyrinth can be drawn with sidewalk chalk outside on a driveway or can be made with masking tape on an inside floor. It can be made portable by painting on several blankets sewn together or may even be permanently constructed with bricks, stones, flowers, or grass.

The center that I cannot find is known to my unconscious mind.
~ W.H. Auden

Enter the labyrinth, walking slowly from the outside into the center on the path created between the lines. Focus on something joyful as you walk. When you reach the center, pause for a moment, then turn and walk the path in reverse order until you reach the outside edge.

SHARE your ideas on how thinking quietly and the feeling of being still can help prepare you for a happy life.

MEMORY

Paraphrasing from Confucius, reflection is the noblest way to learn wisdom. It is a contemplative act which takes past experience and assigns meaning to it. The actual occurrence may seem inconsequential at the time, but given the understanding developed through time and context, it may ultimately be considered one of the profound insights which shapes the individual's life choices. The true power that memory brings is the strength it supplies as the individual realizes s/he has persevered through tough times, and the opportunity it affords to live life in an intentional way. Imagine if each day was approached from the philosophy of "Let's make a memory." What a difference that attitude would make in "mundane" choices!

~ MATERIALS ~
- markers
- pencil
- straight pin
- paper
- scissors
- copies of page 43

Ask the peacemakers to draw an appropriate memorable event as listed on the pinwheel template found on the following page. Cut the pinwheel paper on the dotted lines. Fold each of the quartered sections, bringing the left side of each up to the center of the page. Press the pin through the center of the paper, anchoring all sections. Push the pin containing the pinwheel into the eraser of the pencil.

SHARE favorite memories as well as the memories the peacemakers would like to create.

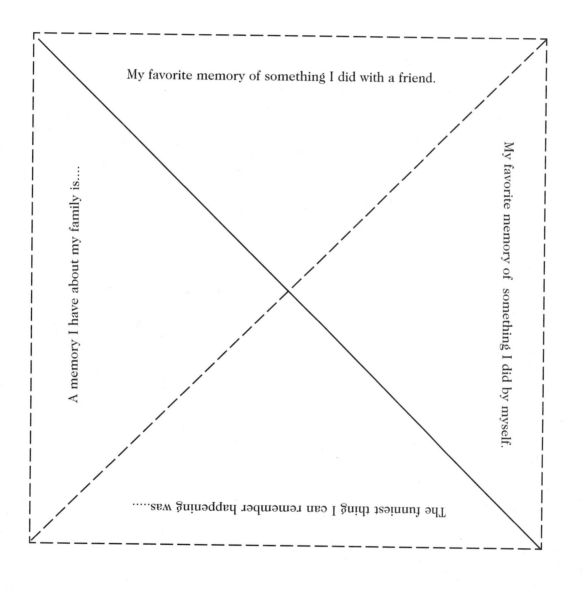

My favorite memory of something I did with a friend.

A memory I have about my family is.....

My favorite memory of something I did by myself.

The funniest thing I can remember happening was......

BOUNCING BLESSINGS

The ability to live through an aura of gratitude is perhaps the strongest motivating factor in life. It means life is approached with expectancy and abundance. It is a hope-filled philosophy which refuses to be satisfied with what is and presses continually for the good that could be. This proactive shift in attitude can be developed and nurtured through a conscious effort to focus on the positive and through the process of expressing gratitude.

~ MATERIALS ~
• balloon

Ask the peacemakers to form a circle and to face each other. Use an inflated balloon to offer up spontaneous expressions of gratitude. As the balloon comes to peacemakers, they will look inside it and imagine something they are thankful for. They will pass the balloon around the circle by bouncing it on fingertips, announcing gratitude at each bounce. The difficulty in controlling the balloon in the desired direction will probably stimulate laughter, which of course contributes significantly to the lesson.

A joyful spirit is evidence of a
grateful heart.
~ Maya Angelou

SHARE YOUR THOUGHTS ...

• Discuss the variety of things named by the peacemakers, including why the participants named the things they did. Were there more possessions, people, or concepts (such as love or happiness) named?

After the discussion, ask the peacemakers to think of the four things they are **MOST** thankful for. Replay the game now that a prioritization has occurred.

THIS WAY, THAT WAY

Goals give direction to life and encourage personal growth. There are many factors which influence the way in which goals are achieved, when they are re-examined, and the merit of each goal.

Internal conviction, or the inner voice and sense of knowing, is an incredibly powerful motivational tool. This type of urging provides the strength to stand up for convictions, the ability to persevere, and the desire to set each standard higher than the last. It is important for the individual to hold on to this authentic and personal power not only to ward off the outside influences which pull a person in different directions, but also to avoid doubt and the negative self-talk which can sabotage even the most noble of goals.

External variables also stimulate and motivate an individual and his/her personal goals. In order to use these elements in beneficial ways, it is important for the individual to be responsive to the outside environment rather than reactive to it. Feedback from others used in a positive way provides information, evaluates and measures progress, and helps the individual gauge effectiveness in reaching their goal.

~ MATERIALS ~
- blindfold
- small object

One person is the sender. The other person is the receiver. The sender's task is to direct the receiver to the goal, the small object placed across the room, using only temperature words for instruction – e.g., "hot" for close, "cold" for the wrong direction.

Blindfold the receiver and carefully spin him/her so that person does not know which direction to go to find the object. Ask the sender to begin giving the hot/warm/cold instructions so that the object can be located. As a group, briefly evaluate how effective the sender and receiver were in their quest for the object.

Repeat in the same way, but this time the receiver will listen VERY carefully and not even take a step until s/he knows the direction for each step. In other words, while standing in place the person will point his/her foot in several directions around his/her body and listen for the temperature word before s/he takes each step. This expression will be more deliberate and should create a direct path to the object.

Once again, as a group, evaluate the effectiveness of reaching the goal. What would have happened if the receiver would have chosen the opposite response and would have refused to listen (covering his/her ears and singing loudly yet still trying to find the object)?

Next, begin the receiver in the same way, but the sender will only be able to use "cold" to direct. How successful was this method in accomplishing the goal? Explain.

Finally, the receiver will have a hidden agenda which no one else knows. The receiver is to do nothing. No matter what the sender says, the receiver is not to move. Notice how the sender reacts. Because the sender's words were not being acknowledged, the person will probably become very frustrated and will stop giving instructions. As a group, assess the effectiveness of this procedure. Hopefully, someone will point out that action has to occur in order to accomplish a goal. The best intentions without follow through will not be successful. Reinforce this truth – Action is a necessary component to growth.

SHARE together times when each person has been successful and unsuccessful in accomplishing a personal goal. What could have made the effort more effective?

TIME IS WHAT IT TAKES

Patience is more than simply the capacity to wait. It is the ability to bear difficulty or hardship without complaint and even with a sense of calm endurance. Yet patience is a relative term. The burden can originate from many causes, both external and internal, such as a profound sense of vision, making timing a matter of perception. Regardless of the degree, the ability to be patient can bring an opportunity for thoughtful response and personal serenity.

~ MATERIALS ~

- spoons
- bowls
- crushed ice
- vanilla
- measuring cup and spoons
- pint-size self-sealing plastic bag
- gallon-size self-sealing plastic bag
- small towel
- rock salt
- milk
- sugar

If you are patient in one moment of anger, you will escape a hundred days of sorrow.
~ Chinese proverb

Place 1 cup milk, 1/2 teaspoon of vanilla, and 2 tablespoons of sugar into the small plastic bag. Remove as much air as possible and seal the end of the bag. Place the filled small bag into the larger plastic bag and add 4 cups of crushed ice and 6 tablespoons of rock salt, surrounding the small bag. Remove the excess air and seal the large bag. Wrap the towel around the outside of the large bag and take turns shaking the bag vigorously. Be patient. With enough shaking you'll have ice cream in a few minutes.

Remove the small bag, wipe the salt water off the outside. Place the ice cream in a bowl and enjoy!

SHARE YOUR THOUGHTS....

- What does it mean to be patient?
- How does patience help when you are trying to learn new things?
- Share an example of a time when you were patient or a time when you were not very patient.
- How does excitement make it harder to be patient?

VALUES UNDER CONSTRUCTION

Values are built through the exercise of choices. When principles are in conflict with each other, a prioritization must be made as to which precept is most important. Values guide actions and determine character. They are formed over the course of a lifetime and they are influenced and shaped by family, friends, and society.

As a group, discuss values.

- What or who influences how you choose to act?
- Where do your values come from?
- How do your values affect your choices?
- What happens when values are in conflict with each other? For instance, what do you do when you value time with your family and getting good grades, but studying keeps you away from those you care about?
- How can you be a positive influence on another's values?

Everyone of us has in him a continent of undiscovered character.
Blessed is he who acts the explorer to his own soul.
~ Author Unknown

DIFFERENT PATHS

Two roads diverged in a wood,
and I – I took the one less traveled by,
and that has made all the difference.
~ Robert Frost ~

There are times in life when a person must choose the level of commitment s/he will live. The illustration as well as the line from the Frost poem depict these types of decisions. The poem reflects the author's gratitude upon reflection of his previous choice, while the picture represents the crossroads of the choice. The individual is alone with his/her decision. As illustrated, the popular way is a well-worn common walk and to simply follow the conventional trail is tempting. The other choice of creating one's own way represents the uncharted territory of a life committed to manifesting the beliefs, attitudes, and values not simply by word, but by deed. A vast amount of energy is required to walk this wilderness path.

The decision to walk the common path is justified with a variety of different reasons. The facts, however, are really quite simple. When faced with the choice, will you compromise your values? The message is clear. The paths are not parallel, they separate into two distinct routes. Will your intentions and your actions be consistent? Will you implement your ideals?

Another way of illustrating this depth of commitment is with chalk, water, and food coloring. You will need both dustless and regular white chalk. To illustrate the easier choice of conforming to minimal societal standards, dip the dustless chalk into the colored water. The chalk will take on the color of the water, but when broken will show that the color was only absorbed on the surface layer and did not have any effect on the inside color of the chalk. To demonstrate the seeker's path, dip the standard chalk into the water. It too changes in color, but when broken will show the color has permeated throughout the chalk. Relate this experiment to the depth of convictions needed to lead a peace-filled life. When put to the test, how true to your intentions are you? Are your convictions a fundamental principle which motivates and transforms your entire life, or are they simply a transitory theory used as an illusion?

FINDERS KEEPERS?

Ethics are values or principles which define what is right and wrong for an individual and society. They set the standard of behavior. For an ethic to have integrity, it must be expressed through consistent conduct, not based upon circumstances. Good intentions are not enough. Actions give credibility to beliefs, attitudes, and values.

~ MATERIALS ~

- marker
- large piece of paper
- picture from page 50

Share the following situation with the peacemakers. You are in a store and realize that you don't have enough money to buy your favorite candy. As you are waiting outside, you notice a lady drop some money. She is walking away. What do you do?

Make a list of all the things that might happen next. Is there one choice that the group considers to be the right thing to do?

Sometimes our choices only affect our lives, but many times our choices affect the lives of other people. Discuss how each choice would affect your life and the lady's life.

SHARE YOUR THOUGHTS...

Explain and discuss the following questions. Notice the acceptable social standard which is supported and held accountable by the group.

- Would your action change if the lady looked as if she might be rich? What if she looked poor and hungry? What if she was crying and came back looking for the money?
- Would your action change if the money was a $100 bill rather than a $5 bill?
- Would your action change if you were sure no one else saw the lady drop the money?
- How do you decide what's the best thing for you to do?
- Does your decision change depending on whether you were the one who lost or found the money? Why or why not?

MY CHOICE, MY DECISION

Some decisions are easy to make because there is a clear choice between a right and wrong alternative. Most choices, however, are harder to make because there are a number of positive options. Taking the time to consider all the options can be a difficult task, but looking at the possibilities leads to sound decisions and positive outcomes.

Postponing a decision until a choice does not have to be made is not a responsible solution – to not make a decision is in itself a decision. The power to choose means there is a responsibility to accept the effects or consequences of the choice.

The choices presented in the following worksheet represent assertive, passive aggressive, accommodating, and avoiding behaviors. Whenever a person acts in an assertive manner, it creates the fairest and best outcome. Assertive behavior simply means thoughts and feelings are expressed in a direct and honest way while ensuring respect for self and others.

~ MATERIALS ~
- pencils
- copy of page 52

Discuss with the peacemakers the importance of considering as many options as possible when making decisions. Stress the value of trying to estimate the possible outcome of each option.

Ask the peacemakers to read each situation on page 52 and to write their responses in the appropriate space. Encourage them to share their responses with the group explaining the reason for the decision.

The distresses of choice are our chances to be blessed.
~ W.H. Arden

SHARE YOUR THOUGHTS...

- Who do you talk to when you need to make a decision?
- Why is it important to think about the different choices when you make a decision?
- Who is responsible for your decision? Tell about a decision that was hard for you to make and how it turned out.
- What usually happens when you try to avoid consequences?

52

MY CHOICE, MY DECISION

Circle your choice for each situation.

SITUATION	MY CHOICE IS...	REASON FOR MY DECISION
Your best friend forgot to study for the big math test. She asks you if you will let her copy from your paper.	• Let her copy my work. • Tell her I'm sorry she forgot to study, but it wouldn't be right to let her copy my answers. • Tell her I'll let her copy, but during the test, I make sure that I keep all the answers covered and impossible to copy. • None of the other answers.	_____ _____ _____ _____ _____ _____
You are invited to two parties at the same time on the same day.	• Go to half of each of the parties. • Choose the party I'd most like to go to and tell the other person I already have plans. • Stay home so no one gets angry then stomp off at school when someone mentions the party. • None of the other answers.	_____ _____ _____ _____
You overhear some of your friends talking about something they don't like about you.	• Ignore it. • Tell your friends your feelings were hurt. • Go to someone else and tell something bad about your friends. • None of the other answers.	_____ _____ _____

THINK AHEAD, THINK IT OUT

For every action, there is a reaction or a consequence. Sometimes the immediate consequence is very small, but over time the consequence may change or grow in its significance. Making positive choices involves considering the possible short-term as well as long-term effects of an action, choosing what reflects personal values and beliefs and understanding the personal motivation or reason for the choice.

~ MATERIALS ~

- scissors
- copy of this page

Make a copy of this page. Cut on the dotted lines to make cards and place them in a pile. Take turns picking a card from the pile. Ask the peacemakers to work together to brainstorm possible consequences of each action. Ask them to consider the immediate effect, then encourage them to consider the long-term consequences of continuing the behavior for a year or for five years.

You compliment your sister or brother	You don't wash your face before bed	You skip breakfast and eat a hamburger and fries for lunch	You never say you're sorry	You read a book instead of watching TV
You don't exercise	You stay up late and watch TV	You practice an instrument	When angry, you stay calm and listen to the other person	You study for your spelling test
You eat foods rich in calcium and vitamins	You do whatever your friend asks	Your friend makes you mad, and you hit them	You forget to feed your dog	You brush and floss your teeth twice each day

SHARE YOUR THOUGHTS...

- Tell about a time when you did something that had a good consequence.
- Is it all right to change your mind and make a different decision if you find out the decision led to a bad consequence? Please give an example.

CHOOSING THE WAY TO PEACE

People create a peaceful world by accepting responsibility and by choosing positive and appropriate attitudes and actions. It is important to recognize patterns of behavior which limit choices. A good decision usually provides the opening for other options rather than the closing off of other opportunities.

Each junction in the maze represents a choice which is available to work for peace. Choose the word that best describes a positive choice and follow the path to peace.

~ MATERIALS ~

• pencils
• copy of this page

First say to yourself what you would be; and then do what you have to do.
~ Epictetus

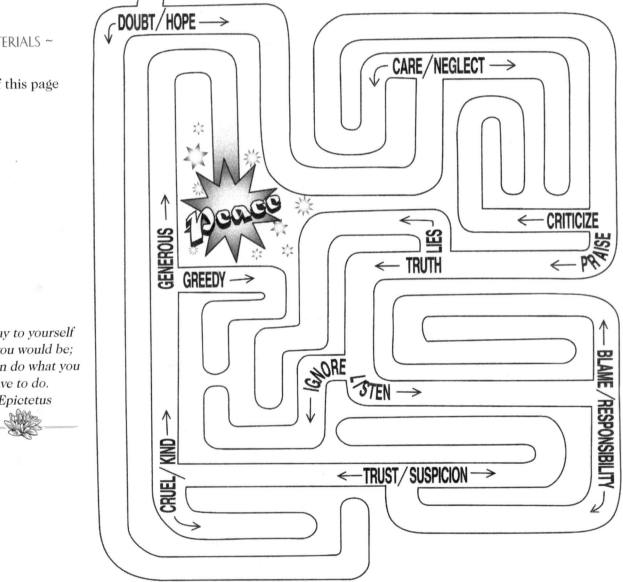

ONE STEP LEADS TO ANOTHER

Attitudes and actions have many wide-ranging ramifications. A choice not only affects the individual but also has an influence on others. As decisions are made, consideration must be given to the effect those choices will have on surrounding people. This effect can be positive or negative and can set up a succession of responses.

~ MATERIALS ~
- large number of dominoes
  or
- small wooden blocks

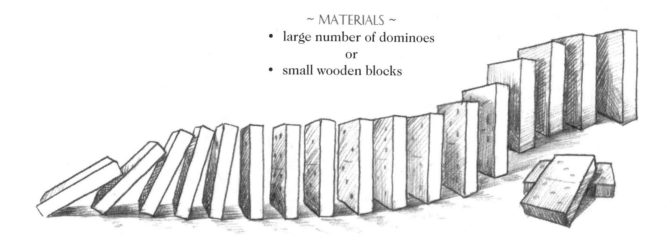

Work together and use the dominoes to create a chain reaction. Set the dominoes up on their ends in a wide variety of patterns and shapes. Tip one domino over to set off a tumbling sculpture. (This is a great illustration of consequences, as even the very young child can see the result of the concept.)

SHARE YOUR THOUGHTS...

- Is one domino more important than another domino? Explain.
- What would happen if we would remove one or two dominoes from the chain?
- What could happen if just one person decided to do something nice for the world?
- Who or what influences you in good or bad ways?

MAKE AN IMPRESSION

With each precious gift of life comes a new being unlike anyone else on earth. Each person has the ability to touch the world in a unique and distinct way. When people have a sense of their worth, they are given the knowledge that their lives truly matter. They have a sense of purpose and are empowered to make the world a better place.

~ MATERIALS ~

- cloth napkin or heavy paperstock
- hammer
- tape
- plant leaves and flowers (Ferns and pansies work well.)

There is no hand so small that it does not leave an imprint on the world.
~ Unknown

Place the paper or cloth on a smooth floor. Arrange the plants on the paper or cloth.

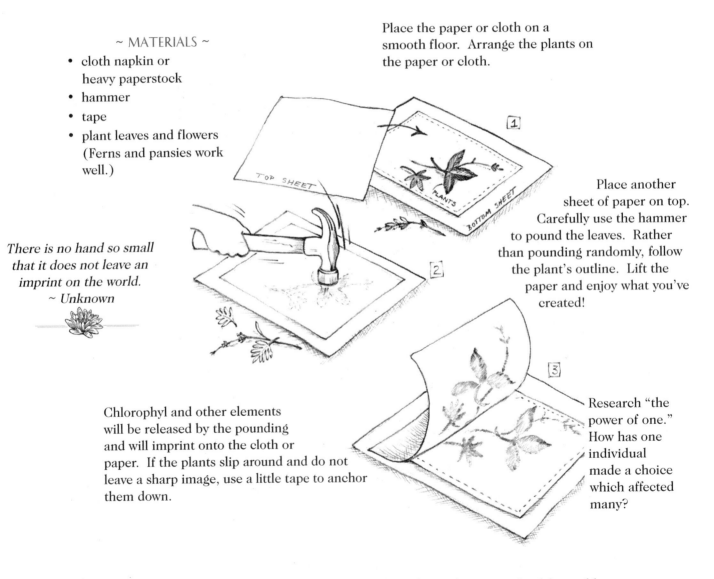

Place another sheet of paper on top. Carefully use the hammer to pound the leaves. Rather than pounding randomly, follow the plant's outline. Lift the paper and enjoy what you've created!

Chlorophyl and other elements will be released by the pounding and will imprint onto the cloth or paper. If the plants slip around and do not leave a sharp image, use a little tape to anchor them down.

Research "the power of one." How has one individual made a choice which affected many?

SHARE with each other about personal worth, times you've felt "of worth," and times you've felt worthless. What responsibility does each person have to make a positive mark on the world?

HEART THOUGHTS

Write your own affirming guided imagery within the heart.

PEACE FOR US

Peace for Us expresses the peacemaking process within our daily relationships. Absolute trust is the foundation for all thriving relationships. This basis provides support and mutual respect and creates inseparable bonds as the individuals grow. A perfect example of this type of trust was demonstrated by my youngest children, Ashley and Drew. Ashley had a loose tooth so she and Drew decided to tie a string around it and pull it out. Drew was only three years old, but he understood the responsibility of the trust level. He watched his sister diligently and only tugged when she raised her hand signalling him to do so. If the pain got too bad, she lowered her hand and he slackened the string immediately. She was the one at risk for hurt so he honored her trust by being especially tender and kind. The tooth never did come out that day, it was simply one of the sweet moments of life.

Interpersonal skills are necessary for relationships to grow. This lesson was also demonstrated in a remarkable way by Ashley and Drew. At the time, our family was practicing the skill of the "I message." Angie and Kristen were becoming very frustrated with Ashley because when they would use the skill, she would simply ignore them. I encouraged the older girls to give her the benefit of the doubt and to keep practicing the positive behavior no matter what response they received because theoretically Ashley, at four, was too young to be capable of using the skill. Then one day, Ashley came home to find her brother had thrown her toys all over and was busily playing with them. She immediately said a perfect "I message" without the aid of any signs as prompts. Her body language was incorrect, and her tone too loud, but the word's meaning struck a chord within her two-year-old brother's heart. He immediately stopped what he was doing, mimicked her body posture with his hands on his hips and began saying, "Ashley, I feel.....I feel.....I feel, Oh, I am so sorry, Ashley." Even though their skill base needed work, they were able to convey to each other the distress, need, and desire to go beyond the problem. They then hugged each other and started playing together. From this time on, we knew the level of ability Ashley was functioning with and held her accountable to be respectful whenever her older sisters applied this skill to their situations.

As Ashley and Drew have grown and committed themselves to practice peacemaking on a daily basis, they have empowered themselves with freedom, laughter, love, kindness, responsibility, and courage. They are truly amazing people!

SHELTERING TREE

Mahali Safi is Swahili for "place of peace," or "a good place," or "sanctuary." Everyone needs a personal Mahali Safi - a place to feel safe, secure, at home, and sheltered from the scary things of the world. This sense of being grounded is a primal need and the first step in establishing positive self-worth as well as the ability to connect with others.

It is in the shelter of each other that the people live.
~ Irish proverb

By listing the people who make up their "sheltering tree," the peacemakers will be labeling those they can trust. When they then have an unexpected need, they have already identified people they can go to for help.

Share the meaning of Mahali Safi. Make copies of the following page and ask the peacemakers to draw themselves somewhere under the tree. In the spaces provided within the tree branches, instruct the peacemakers to write the names of people they trust and who protect or comfort them when they are in need. Examples would be a parent, sibling, friend, teacher, neighbor, or whoever the child feels is a safe person with whom to share.

Use the metaphors of wind and rain to illustrate the hazards and harm groups of kind people can protect themselves from. Talk about how people are individuals similar to individual branches of a tree, but are all united in the same source. Perhaps they would then like to label what they think holds everyone together. Is it love? Shared experiences? You'll be surprised at the depth of consciousness.

SHARE YOUR THOUGHTS...

- Tell another peacemaker about the people on your tree and how they are supportive.
- Tell about a time when someone listed on your tree made you feel good about yourself.
- Take this picture to someone you listed and tell that person why you named him/her on your sheltering tree.

FRIENDSHIP BRACELET

Deep within the human psyche lies a longing, a need to connect. Friends give resonance to life. They provide the opportunity for the individual to be in relationship, to be close, to belong. Humans are social creatures, needing the companionship and acceptance that only tapping into the vibrational energy of another human being can provide. Group interaction is an emotional necessity, and provides an accountability factor for ethics, essential encouragement for reaching personal goals, support through difficult times, and a source of collaboration for societal improvement.

~ MATERIALS ~

- tongue depressor
- paper punch
- 1/4 inch wide ribbon
- water
- glass
- paint
- paint brush
- spray-on polyurethane
- scissors

This is a rather involved craft.

Each peacemaker should make two friendship bracelets.

Hold a true friend with both your hands.
~ Nigerian proverb

To make the tongue depressor pliable, soak it in water for several hours. Using the paper punch, put a hole near each end while it is still wet. Place it inside a round drinking glass and leave it for several hours until dry to give it shape. Decorate it with paint and seal it with spray-on polyurethane. Cut a piece of ribbon about six inches long and run it through each hole. Give one bracelet to your friend and keep one for yourself. Tie the ribbon into a bow after placing the bracelet on your wrist. Tell your friend three things you like about him/her.

SHARE YOUR THOUGHTS....

- What makes a good friend?
- How can you be a good friend to others?
- How do you make new friends?

COUNT ON ME

A true friend isn't simply around during the good times, they are available when there is a need to help out.

GIVE ME A HAND

Two peacemakers will sit on the floor one directly behind the other one. The front person puts his/her arms behind his/her back and grabs his/her own elbows. The back person scoots up closely behind his/her friend and inserts his/her arms between the elbow and body of the front person. The back person will be directed by the front person and serve as the arms for fun activities. The back person will close his/her eyes, listen and follow the front person's directions. Some ideas to do – drawing a picture, using blocks to build a tower, frosting a cookie and feeding it to the front person.

Please respect an individual's sense of personal space and don't ask them to participate if they find this activity intrusive.

STAND BY ME

Two peacemakers will sit on the floor back to back. The pair will hook elbows and then work together to come to a standing position without releasing their arms.

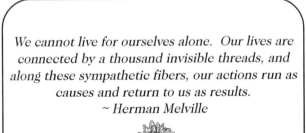

We cannot live for ourselves alone. Our lives are connected by a thousand invisible threads, and along these sympathetic fibers, our actions run as causes and return to us as results.
~ Herman Melville

SHARE YOUR THOUGHTS...

- If you had to define or explain what a friend was to someone who didn't understand the concept, what would you say?
- Give an example of a time when you needed a friend and someone was willing to help.
- Share an example of a time when you were willing to help a friend.

GIVING GIFTS

Unspoken sentiments need to be voiced. The simplest words can convey the deepest meaning when spoken to a person for what could be considered common actions. It is easy to forget these courtesies in day-to-day life, "Thank you... I appreciate you... You did a good job," yet when remembered they can mean so much.

~ MATERIALS ~
- pipe cleaners
- tissue paper
- scissors
- paper punch

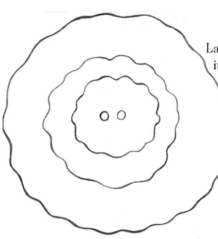

Layer the tissue paper on top of itself and cut several circles of at least three different sizes. Using single sheets, place the different sized circles one on top of another as shown. Use the paper punch to make two holes in the center of the tissue paper.

Loop the pipe cleaner through the layers of tissue paper. Gently mold the tissue into a flower shape as the pipe cleaner is twisted to make a stem. Repeat the process to create a bouquet.

Give your bouquet to someone who quietly goes about life doing nice things. Tell them you are thankful for the things they do and the person they are.

SHARE YOUR THOUGHTS...

- Why is saying "Thank you" important?
- List some ways you can share your appreciation with others.
- Tell about a time when someone surprised you with an unexpected gift.

WEIGHT OF THE WORLD

Independence is a valuable trait, but interdependence is even more commendable as it maintains the identity of the individual while recognizing the importance of the community. To need assistance is not a deficiency or failure, but simply the acknowledgement that some things are too large for capable individuals to handle alone. The ability to ask for help without feeling indebted is a quality which all people need to learn. The readiness to accept the offering of help is an opportunity to learn to receive the gift with grace and dignity.

~ MATERIALS ~
- rock
- marking pen
- old coat with extra pockets

Advanced preparation is needed to make the coat. Use an old coat and sew extra pockets all over the outside.

Ask the peacemakers to write down a problem, worry, or concern on a rock. As each person takes his/her turn trying on the coat, the other peacemakers will slowly and carefully fill the pockets announcing the burden as they place the rock. The increasing weight of the coat will illustrate how "heavy" our problems become when we try to carry them by ourselves.

I believe the problems of human destiny are
not beyond the reach of human beings.
~ John F. Kennedy

SHARE YOUR THOUGHTS ...

- Why is it important to ask for help when you need it?
- How does sharing a problem make it seem easier to bear?
- Share about a time when you helped someone or someone helped you.

ANOTHER VIEW

A person's reality is shaped by his/her conscious knowledge, life experience, and range of understanding. The individual's capacity for insight is filtered through his/her philosophy, viewpoint, and personal investment. Two people can examine the same data and arrive at completely divergent conclusions. Yet each interpretation is real and represents truth to the individual. The ability to suspend judgement and to look at a circumstance through another person's point of view is a useful tool which expresses consideration and respect.

~ MATERIALS ~

- scissors
- page 66
- enlargement tool –
  copy machine or overhead projector

Say not, "I have found the truth,"
*but rather, "I have found **A** truth."*
~ Kahlil Gibran

Cut the pictures found on page 66 apart and enlarge them so that everyone can see them. Show each picture separately and have the group decide whose eyes they are looking through. In other words, they now have the ability to see the world from someone else's point of view. Who could they be?

Answers – a fish looking through its bowl
            an eagle or hawk from its tree
            a mouse on the floor
            a bat in a cave

Another fun activity would be to write about a common object from different perspectives. For instance, describe what a tree would be like to a bird, a squirrel, a ladybug, or a cicada. Remember, they can only describe the tree from their point of view.

SHARE YOUR THOUGHTS...

- Describe the different points of view represented in the pictures.
- Why is it important to consider another person's point of view?
- How can people do a better job understanding what may be true or real to one person may or may not be true or real to another person?

ALL ANGLES CONSIDERED

Decisions made based upon consensus are stronger conclusions because they allow for a variety of perceptions to be expressed. Consensus occurs when individual agendas are suspended and each person actively seeks to understand another person's point of view, ideas, and desires. It is participatory in nature. It is not majority rule and does not involve the taking of a vote. To base an agreement on consensus means the time has been taken to tap into the collective consciousness in order to seek out a decision which is best for all. It is not only a meeting of minds, but a meeting of hearts. Consensus establishes a covenant or bond between the people involved as each has the capacity to stand up for the agreement because of their personal investment and validation of the process.

~ MATERIALS ~
• copy of page 68

Show view number one (going from left to right) of an object from page 68 and ask the peacemakers if they can reach agreement on what the object is. Ask them to share all the ideas of what it could be. If they can't reach agreement, show them views one and two together, once again having them announce possibilities of what it could be. If they need a third view, show all three views at once; now they will probably be able to agree on what the object is. Continue in this way with all the pictures on the sheet.

ANSWERS
a scissors
a cup
a key

A mind that is stretched by a new idea can
never go back to its original dimensions.
~ Oliver Wendell Holmes

SHARE YOUR THOUGHTS...

• How easy was it to decide what the object was with only one way of looking at it?
• How did your group decide what the objects were? How did you reach agreement? Were you respectful in the process?
• Why is it important in your life to consider looking at a problem from another person's point of view?

68

SEEING POSSIBILITIES

Perspective provides the chance to look at a situation with "new eyes." There are times when an individual is too close to a situation and needs a different opinion or interpretation. When another viewpoint is considered, new options may suddenly appear. Differing views do not necessarily mean one point of view is "right" and the other view is "wrong." They are simply not alike.

~ MATERIALS ~
  • page 70

Mr. Peace

Show the peacemakers each of the "optical illusions" found on page 70. In some cases (in order to see the desired effect) the page may need to be turned in different directions, or someone who sees the hidden item may need to carefully point it out to someone who can't see it.

*Every man takes the limits of his own field
of vision for the limits of the world.*
~ Arthur Schopenhauer

SHARE YOUR THOUGHTS...

• How easy was it for you to see clearly when looking at the optical illusions? Please explain.
• How does looking at something from only one perspective or point of view create mistakes and misinterpretations?
• How can you invite others to share their points of view when there is a problem to solve?

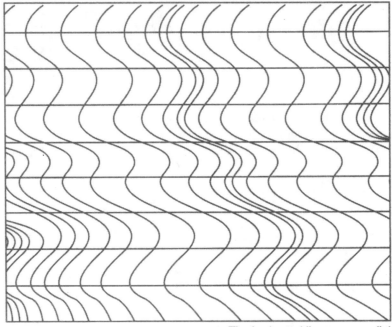

The horizontal lines are parallel

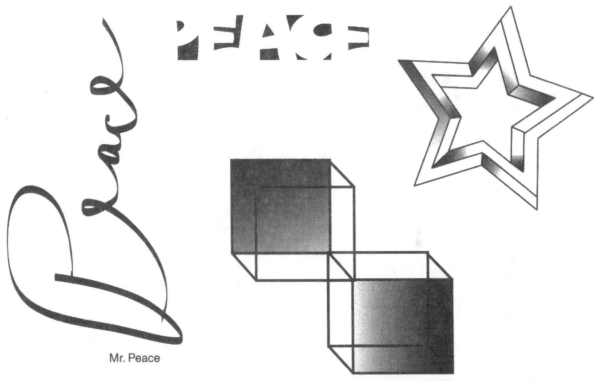

Mr. Peace

Which gray section is in the foreground?

PERSPECTICALS

The way a person perceives and responds to a situation relates more to the person's attitudes than to the actual circumstances. Attitude is a conscious state of mind, a prevailing disposition which colors and filters the way in which the individual views her/himself. It also determines a person's readiness to respond to others. This power of approach can set the stage for effective interpersonal relations when the stance is open and receptive.

~ MATERIALS ~

- scissors
- glue
- construction paper
- 5 pairs of inexpensive sunglasses

Ask the peacemakers to divide into 5 small groups. Give each group a pair of glasses and one of the following attitudes: fear, love, jealousy, acceptance, or suspicion. Instruct each group to work together to decorate the glasses so that the glasses represent the assigned attitude.

Discuss what it means to look at circumstances from different attitudes and how one's way of viewing a situation affects individual choices. Have each team role play one of the specified situations by acting it out from the perspective of the team's glasses. Ask other teams to share their points of view from the perspective of the team's glasses. You may need to help people get started, but they will catch on and soon will be able to quickly see things from several different points of view and will understand how attitude colors everything we see.

~ SITUATIONS ~

- Your neighbor's dog is barking at you.
- A new family moves in next door.
- You ask a friend for help with homework.
- Your friend gets a new bike.
- You and a friend are both trying out for a school team.

SHARE YOUR THOUGHTS...

- How do your feelings change when you see a situation from a different attitude?
- How does changing your attitude affect the way you act?

THE ANSWER IS UP TO YOU

People have their own outlooks on life which are influenced by how they perceive the world. This personal vision is based on beliefs, awareness, experiences, traditions, associations, and circumstances. New concepts can be discovered and shared when people enlarge their scope of the truth by genuinely seeking out and considering the impressions of others.

~ MATERIALS ~

- pencils
- crayons or paints
- copies of pages 72 - 74

Instruct the peacemakers to choose at least one of the pictures found on pages 72 - 74. The peacemakers will finish each drawing and will then colorize it, using the crayons or paints.

Each drawing has a base on which to begin. What the picture will end up as is up to the individual completing the scene. For instance, is the person at the top of page 73 a male or female? What ethnic group is this person? Is the person picnicking, praying, planting flowers or engaged in some other activity? The answer is up to the peacemaker.

SHARE the completed pictures with each other.

Wonder at the unique expression each person has given the image.

Talk about how we "answer" life's questions everyday by the way in which we choose to look at the situation, to think, and to act.

Discuss how these individual responses help or hurt others.

Make a plan for answering life's questions with a "Yes, I can" outlook.

*We don't see things as they
are, we see them as we are.*
~ Anais Nin

BODY LANGUAGE

Statistics vary, but it is estimated that approximately 70% of all communication is delivered through body language; just over 20% is conveyed through intonation and inflection; and less than 10% is transmitted through spoken words. The voice may say one thing, but a conflicting message may be conveyed through mannerisms, postures, and gestures. Sometimes this unspoken language can be misunderstood. If a person is standing with arms crossed, does it mean that the person is closed off, or does it simply mean the person is physically cold?

~ MATERIALS ~
- paper
- pencil
- scissors
- copies of page 76

Show each picture found on page 76 to the peacemakers and have them guess how each person in the picture is feeling. Which people would they like to be around? Why? Discuss what prompted them to make a decision when they don't know the people pictured and haven't heard what has been said. Individuals might like to discuss a time when they felt the same way as someone in the picture.

Next, ask everyone to write a feeling word down on a piece of paper (*e.g.*, kind, happy, grouchy, proud). Cut the words apart and place in a pile. Each person will take a turn acting out the word written on the paper. Participants are not allowed to make any noises but to simply use their bodies to communicate the words.

*I found things I could say with color and
shapes that I couldn't say in any other
way...things I had no words for.*
~ Georgia O'Keeffe

SHARE YOUR THOUGHTS...

- Was it easy or hard to understand each other when you couldn't use words? Please explain.
- Describe how your voice and body can partner together to help people communicate better.

HIDDEN MESSAGE

The pitch, tone, rhythm, and emphasis of the voice all give meaning to the spoken word. A single pitch or monotone voice can suggest a meditative chant or a lecture in which concentration becomes difficult, while an animated voice can stress the importance of whatever point is being made. Without even seeing the person or knowing the words, a statement in which the pitch rises at the end is interpreted as a question.   Clues on the level of investment as well as to the purpose of the message are expressed through voice inflection and intonation.

~ MATERIALS ~

- small white candle such as a birthday candle
- watercolor paints
- paint brush
- paper
- water
- small container for water

Tear the pieces of paper into fun shapes such as hearts, etc. Write a secret message on the paper using the candle. The message should be something nice. Brush the extra wax off the paper. Give your paper to a friend. As your friend water colors over the paper, the message will appear.

From the emergence of tone comes the
divergence of thought.
~ Visions of Gregorian Chants

SHARE YOUR THOUGHTS...

- Demonstrate what your voice sounds like when you are feeling excited, angry, proud, mean, silly, or tired.
- What are three things you can do when you are listening to make sure you understand the meaning behind the words?

I CAN'T HEAR WHAT YOU SAY

Communication skills are not innate; they must be learned and practiced for effective interaction to occur. True communication means the message is not simply heard, but understood. Thus, comprehension is based more on experience than vocabulary. Nonverbal communication is traditionally associated with body posture and gesture, distance, facial expression, and tone of voice. This exercise, however, establishes the concept of action as a nonverbal communicative tool.

~ MATERIALS ~
- modeling clay or dough
- flash cards
- watch or clock

Modeling dough
1 cup flour
1/2 cup salt
2 teaspoons cream of tartar
1 cup water
1 tablespoon vegetable oil

Mix together. Place in a pan, cook and stir on low heat until thick and lumpy. Turn the mixture out onto wax paper and when it is cool enough knead until smooth.

Prior to the activity, make two sets of identical flash cards. Write a common item on each flash card. Examples might be a cup, fork, trumpet, fish, etc.

Divide the peacemakers into two teams. Each team will work together to guess as many flash cards as possible in a 3-minute time frame. The word on the flash card will be communicated only by making the item with the modeling clay.

Live truth instead of professing it.
~ Elbert Hubbard

SHARE YOUR THOUGHTS...

- How easy or difficult was it to communicate the card's message using only the action of sculpting with clay?
- If someone were to say s/he liked you, but acted as if s/he didn't, which message would you believe? Why?
- Explain how actions can give meaning to words, ideas, and feelings.

MESSAGE SPINNERS

Misinterpretation is the foremost communication problem. Even with direct communication, the margin for misunderstanding is immense. The extent to which intention and meaning can be twisted when indirect communication methods are used is boundless. Each person deserves to be heard from a first-person perspective. Rumor, innuendo, hearsay, and other indirect approaches only advance comprehension errors by distorting and confusing the initial message. In other words, facts and motivations can get confused and all turned around creating an entirely different interpretation of the message which is unfair to the originator of the message. Choosing not to participate in indirect communication patterns is a healthy and mature decision which aids the day-to-day work of peacemaking.

~ MATERIALS ~

- rubber bands
- lightweight piece of cardboard
- pencil
- paper punch
- scissors

Prior to the activity, draw a circle on a piece of cardboard approximately 1 1/2 inches in diameter. Cut out the circle. Make enough cardboard discs so that each peacemaker has two.

Instruct the peacemakers to use the paper punch to put holes in the cardboard disc and then attach a rubber band through each hole as shown.

In the center of the disc, each peacemaker will draw objects which are paired together, placing one half of each pair on the two sides of the disc. For instance, on one side of the disc a fish bowl might be drawn. On the opposite side of the same disc, a fish might be drawn. (The top of one side of the disc is the bottom of the opposite side.) Other paired examples might include a bird and a nest, a tiger and a cage, etc.

When the drawings are complete, the peacemaker will hold a rubber band in each hand and have a friend rotate the disc several times so that the rubber band twists around itself. When the disc is released, the spinning of the disc will create an animation effect merging the two items. For instance, it will appear as if the fish is now in the fish bowl.

The reverse side also has a reverse side.
~ Japanese proverb

SHARE YOUR THOUGHTS....

- How can you help to make sure that the words people say are understood?
- What should you do if someone is talking about someone else and telling others what that person supposedly said?

READ MY MIND

Conjecture and assumption take the place of comprehension when communication skills break down. The result can be confusion, misunderstanding, and even severe hurt. Telepathy is not a reliable way to exchange information; mind reading is not part of the skill base! This facetious statement is made only to point out the necessity of clear communication. Meaning as well as thought needs to be transferred. When intention is understood, many times the hurt is immediately softened and the offense forgiven simply because of the realization there was never the desire to cause pain, but merely a breakdown of communication skills. The message's sender and receiver are both responsible for working together until the correct interpretation is conveyed.

~ MATERIALS ~
- 8 playing cards

The peacemakers will take turns picking a card while another peacemaker is out of the room. When the "psychic" peacemaker enters the room, the dealer will touch each card and ask which card is the chosen card. (While each card is touched, the dealer asks very quickly, "Is it this one, this one, this one, etc.") The "psychic" peacemaker, much to the amazement of everyone else, will guess correctly every time.

The secret to the trick which is known to both the dealer and the "psychic" before the activity begins is in the layout of the cards. The cards will be laid out as shown. Only one 8 will be on the table. The other peacemakers can pick any of the cards, the dealer communicates their choices to the psychic when touching each card before the guess. The dealer touches the number 8 card at the point on the face of the card which signals the place on the table of the chosen card.

Repeat several times, each time allowing a different peacemaker to choose a card. They will try to guess what kind of communication is going on between the dealer and the psychic, but will probably not be successful.

Chosen card is communicated to psychic by dealer's touch on number 8 card.

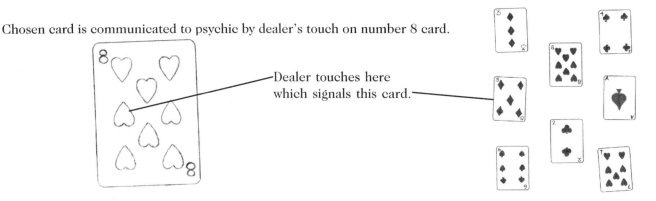

Dealer touches here which signals this card.

SHARE the secret of the trick with everyone. Then talk about how there had to be a trick for this type of clear communication of thought to occur. Talk about times in life when clear communication doesn't happen because people expect others to know what they are thinking. What can help people understand each other and avoid problems?

TALK ABOUT IT

The ability to identify, express and take responsibility for individual feelings, wants and needs in a way which does not blame or accuse another is a valuable skill. The "I message" is a simple tool which facilitates this individual empowerment and affects positive dialog where mutual respect is honored. Proficiency only comes with practice but over time this technique, which at first may seem awkward, becomes a matter of habit.

The "I message" has been proven effective in aiding the communicative process. At first, this skill building will need the aid of a prompt as found on page 82 where the individual descriptions can be added. Think of it as a recipe card. As abilities improve, the prompt won't be needed and the feelings, needs, and wants will be voiced in a natural style.

Practice giving "I messages" using the following situations –

- Your sister keeps making annoying noises while you are trying to do your homework.

- Your friend is mad at you because you chose another friend to take skating.

- You keep tripping on your dad's shoes by the front door.

- You really want to talk to your mom but she keeps ignoring you.

- Your friend ignored you in the hall.

- Your sister borrowed your skirt and put a hole in it.

- The dog chewed on your stuffed animal when your brother was supposed to be watching him.

82

The "I" message

I feel _____ (feeling word)

When you _____ (describe the behavior)

Because I _____ (how it has affected me)

I would like _____ (what I need or want)

If a person is not sincere in his/her use of the "I message" or simply not yet able to apply it properly, it may be manipulated and become a tool which avoids responsibility and assigns blame. An example of this would be on the second line where rather than describing the behavior, the other person would be attacked. This change from an "I" message to a "You" message is not at all helpful and needs to be recognized as a harmful shift.

Change the misapplication, correcting the statement from a "You" statement back into the productive "I" statement.

• I feel angry that you act like a jerk because I get mad. I would like you to give me the baseball.

• I feel hurt when you never listen to me or appreciate what I am doing because I think you don't care about me. I would like it if you would shut up.

• I feel like you are embarrassing in public when you act stupid because I think you're so obnoxious. I would like it if you would be a normal person.

SHARE AND CARE

~ MATERIALS ~
- tape
- place marker
- dice (1 die)
- copy of pages 83 & 84

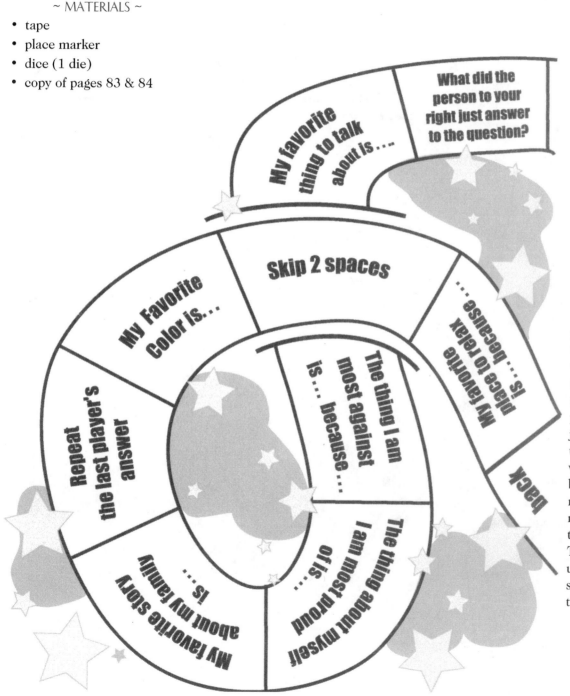

What did the person to your right just answer to the question?

My favorite thing to talk about is . . .

Skip 2 spaces

My Favorite Color is . . .

My favorite place to relax is . . . because . . .

The thing I am most against is . . . because . . .

Repeat the last player's answer

The thing about myself I am most proud of is . . .

My favorite story about my family is . . .

back

Tape the copy of pages 83 & 84 together to form the gameboard. Provide each peacemaker with a marker to move around the gameboard (jelly bean, coin, etc.). Each player may begin at any square and may move either way around the path. Roll the die to determine the number of spaces to move. After landing on a square, the player completes the thought or does whatever action is required by that square. When a player completes the journey and returns to the square on which the player began, the person moves his/her marker to a star on the outer perimeter. The game is not over until everyone is on a star and can join in the celebration.

SHARE & CARE

Communication is one of the most important basic life skills. Many hours are spent learning to read and write, comparatively little time is spent learning the skills of speaking and listening. Unless discussion skills are developed effectively and practiced periodically, it is very hard to understand another person and to work out problems. Listening with the heart is a vital key to peacemaking.

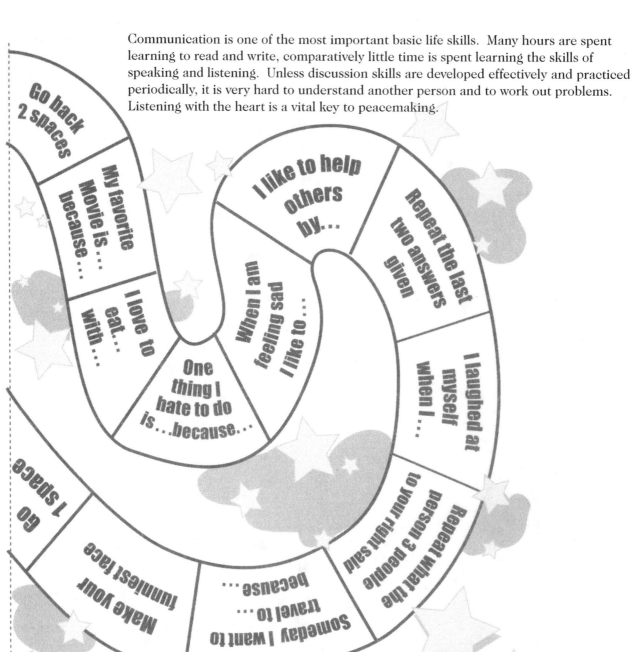

STICKS & STONES

"Sticks and stones can break my bones, but words can never hurt me." This anonymous chant has often been used as a response to name calling or to other taunting. The idea behind it, of course, is that a person should ignore the unkind words and not allow them to define the personhood. In theory, there is truth to the saying, but in reality, there is nothing more potentially damaging than cruel words. Words can be used as brutal weapons, demeaning the very essence of the person, undermining the individual's self-esteem, and jeopardizing the person's sense of dignity. They may act as dream crushers and can create a woundedness which far outlasts the assault. Of course, people who are continually negative or who seem to delight in bullying are enmeshed in pain themselves; rather than engage in the difficult job of self-reflection, they vent their hostilities at others.

It is interesting to note that sticks and stones are not harmful in and of themselves; rather it is how people choose to use them which determines whether they are beneficial or damaging.

Words have the ability to build bridges or to erect walls, depending on how they are used. Verbal communication is an important tool in the peace process as it can create awareness and can help clarify intentions in misunderstandings.

Sticks and stones will break our bones,
but words will break our hearts.
~ Robert Fulghum

PARAPHRASING is a tool which empowers words to release their potential for good. It is an affirming technique which assists people in knowing that they have not only been heard, but understood.

The art of paraphrasing is accomplished by listening attentively to what the other person is saying and then by repeating what you understood the other person to say in your own words. It is not simply mimicking back the exact words like a tape recorder; rather, it is a restating which allows each person to listen for meaning and to make sure the correct interpretation has been conveyed.

Divide into pairs. One person will give an "I message" and the second person will paraphrase the statement.

As a group, discuss the value and possible uses of this skill.

UP AGAINST THE WALL

When people are feeling the need to guard their thoughts and opinions, they are not able to enter the communication process free of barriers. The need to defend and protect creates a resistance to exploring another person's point of view and establishes a distance between the individuals attempting to communicate. The defensive or fixed position may even degenerate into a hostile environment in which no one feels heard and respected.

To confront simply means to seek the truth. For honest communication and truth seeking to occur, the participants must feel centered in a trust relationship where ideas are freely shared and different opinions are valued.

Stand sideways against the wall with your left shoulder and left foot touching it. Remaining in that position, try to lift your right foot.   As long as your left foot and shoulder are held firmly against the wall you won't be able to lift the other leg. This is because to stand on one leg, a shift in the center of gravity must be made so all the weight is over that leg. When one side of the body is against the wall, the shift cannot be made onto that leg because the wall is in the way.

You cannot shake hands with a clenched fist.
~ Indira Gandhi

SHARE in a discussion about how if people do not believe they have real options for expressing their views, they can feel as if they are trapped in a corner with no place to go. Associate this with times when people have become angry for no apparent reason.

• What needs to happen when someone does not think his/her ideas are being heard?
• What can be done to build trust in a relationship so that everyone feels safe to share thoughts and opinions?
• How can listening to another person's ideas help you to understand the situation more clearly?

WALLS & BRIDGES

Healthy relationships have conflicts. They are simply a fact of life. Hopefully though, the conflicts are constructive in nature, valuing different opinions and producing more honest, caring, balanced, and fulfilled connections. Sometimes though, the conflict can be destructive causing misunderstanding and distrust between people. The climate becomes accusatory and there is a need to "win" the disagreement or prove a point. A person can be "right" and still be alone because the relationship has been broken.

The integrity of a bridge, or link, is based on every piece being true to its intention. A reorientation into a win/win mentality is essential as is the commitment to work together diligently for unity. It is important to practice effective communication. Perhaps one person is deeply hurt, and the other is totally clueless about the pain. The seemingly trivial things need to be addressed. Without fair resolution, these little points may build up and hold unrealistic significance. When there is a sincere desire to get along combined with a competent skill base, tense situations can actually turn into times of incredible growth due to the choices of the participating individuals.

~ MATERIALS ~
- pencils
- copies of pages 88 & 89

On the bricks of the wall found on page 88, write the things which can come between people and destroy relationships. They can be attitudes, words, or actions.

On the stones of the bridge found on page 89, write the things which can bring people together. Once again, they can be attitudes, words, or behaviors.

It is from numberless diverse acts of courage and belief that human history is shaped. Each time a man stands up for an ideal, or acts to improve the lot of others, or strikes out against injustice, he sends forth a tiny ripple of hope, and crossing each other from a million different centers of energy and daring, those ripples build a current that can sweep down the mightiest walls of oppression and resistance.
~ Robert F. Kennedy

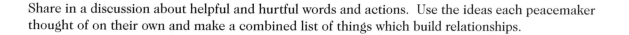

Share in a discussion about helpful and hurtful words and actions. Use the ideas each peacemaker thought of on their own and make a combined list of things which build relationships.

WALLS

BRIDGES

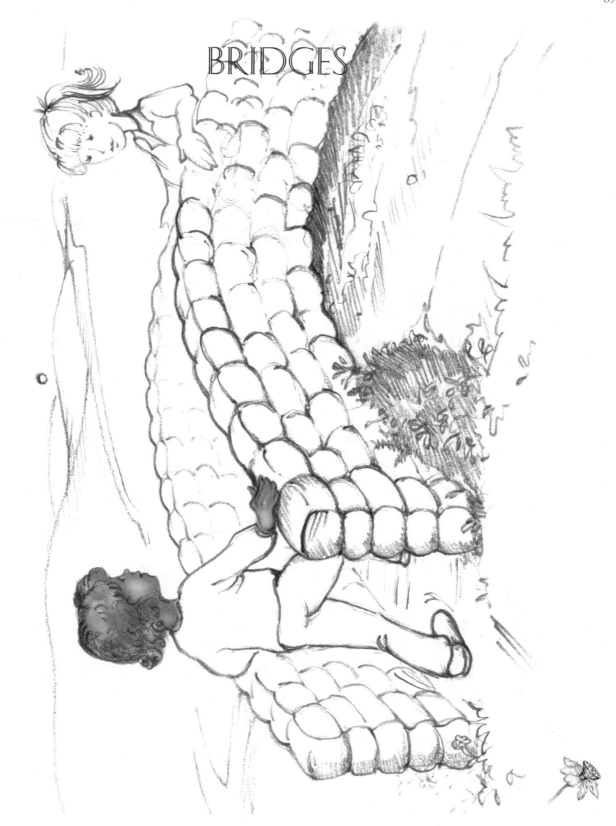

TALK TO EACH OTHER

When there is hurt between people, it often leads to more pain and frustration because no one knows quite what the problem is. The antonym of frustrate is facilitate. The way to facilitate a recovery in a relationship is to talk to each other about individual needs, thoughts, and feelings. The responsibility to fix the problem lies with everyone involved. Be transparent with one another.

If you have offended someone, you will need to go to that person and ask for his/her forgiveness. To ask forgiveness signifies you are committed to changing the offending behavior and working towards a wholeness in the relationship.

If you are hurt, you need to take the time and examine the hurt and decide whether or not you are offended. It may be that upon examination, you will understand the other person's intent and know they meant no harm. Forgiveness is natural when you understand the pain caused was completely unintentional. If upon examination, you decide you are offended, however, you need to go to that person and tell them of your distress. S/he may be totally unaware of how you feel. Taking the time to share with each other will advance the healing and lead to reconciliation. Our actions don't always express the essence of who we really are, but with patience, compassion, and love, true understanding is possible.

Not everything that is faced can be changed...but...nothing can be changed until it is faced.
~ James Baldwin

THE ROAD LESS TRAVELED

When there is a disagreement, traditional patterns of behavior based upon a "survival of the fittest" mentality demand the establishment of "sides" where one party is the winner or "right." The subtleties of higher level learning engage peacemaking skills in the area of communication which many times prevent or disarm a destructive conflict.

When faced with a disagreement, which road will you choose? The common way, or the way of the peacemaker, which brings mutual understanding to the situation?

On pages 92 and 93, two different "walks" are illustrated through an encounter of two people and their dogs. In each exchange, the stimulus is the same and ideas are presented, however, the results couldn't be more different.

The man and the woman each like taking their dogs out for a walk. When they meet each other they begin a discussion and at some point in the conversation find they have personal opinions which are different.

The common path is found on page 92. The difference of opinion is discovered (in this case a preference for big or small dogs). Rather than be comfortable in the tension of opposites, the conversation becomes one which begins to have an agenda of comparison and proving that one view is "right" and the other view is "wrong."

The "**proving**" mentality creates a judgement and an adversarial stance between the two people. It is based upon a concept that one way of thinking is better than another and is very much rooted in winning and losing in a debate style.

As illustrated, the gentleman begins to state his case in a way to convince the woman that big dogs are better. He believes, judging from his body language and facial expression, that he is simply demonstrating the superiority of his choice and once the woman sees the obvious she too will be convinced. By defending his position, he effectively alienates the woman.

Now, the woman being of the same mindset, begins to prove her position. She has felt threatened by his claim of "Big dogs are better" and begins a process of building her case favoring little dogs by diminishing the abilities and traits of the larger animal.

At the end of the discussion, no true understanding has been reached and the two leave unchanged, or many times worse than before the interplay began.

On page 93, we find the illustration of the path few have the courage to take. The setup to the situation is identical, but the two players are content to suspend judgement and the competitive attitude and experience a new way of being.

In this instance an element of sharing is present as each individual releases his/her own agenda in order to understand the perspective of another. The different view is no longer considered an opposing view, simply a different way of thinking.

The "**sharing**" attitude creates a space where vulnerability is honored and protected. Open exploration follows a respectful path which allows for the assertion of different viewpoints through honest questioning, respectful dialog, and mutual appreciation.

In this instance the two will continue with their affinity to their personal preference of big or little dogs, but they leave the exchange acknowledging a newfound value within the opinion of another.

It is significant to note each contributing factor; the internal motivation, the way of presenting point of view, and the outcome are all different in this model due to the personal risk, skill, and positive actions of each person.

PROVING

EXCHANGE LEADS TO
DIFFERENCE OF OPINION

DEFEND POSITION

DIMINISH OTHER

LEAVE UNCHANGED

SHARING

EXCHANGE LEADS TO
DIFFERENCE OF OPINION

HONEST QUESTIONING

RESPECTFUL DIALOG

*Do not follow where the
path may lead. Go,
instead, where there is
no path and leave a trail.
~ Ralph Waldo Emerson*

MUTUAL APPRECIATION

BUILDING BRIDGES

Bridges to Understanding is a three-dimensional keystone bridge which teaches and empowers people to solve their problems through creative and collaborative means. It takes the abstract concept of peacemaking into real and practical terms. The steps delineated on the blocks of the bridge are reinforced throughout this text and can be used to complement each other as a way of introducing and practicing a specific skill.

By working together to actually build a physical structure from opposing sides, the peacemakers understand each side is responsible for half the work. It is an individual choice, which determines if the steps are going to be followed and therefore accepted into the process. Because of this commitment, the collaborative steps literally come together and are delineated in the remaining blocks.

The blocks serve as prompts for the comprehensive process:

CALM DOWN, AND COOL OFF – reminds peacemakers to take responsibility for themselves and the situation rather than assigning blame and making the problem worse. It activates the mind and provides the opportunity to respond, not simply react, with a conscious choice to participate in the process. By centering, the individual is open to an attitude of collaboration and consents to giving his/her very best to the effort.

AGREE TO RESPECT – approaches the problem from the standpoint that all people deserve respect. It is not something which is earned, it is a right and as such will not be violated. This is more difficult than it would seem as "normal" and acceptable behavior is loaded with subtle actions of disrespect. Everyone is important and equal in the process, therefore value of personhood is expressed. This block is additionally important because more often than not, the problem is not about the real issue, but rather symptomatic of deeper imbalances.

SAY FACTS AND FEELINGS – requires a self-knowledge about what the individual is feeling, as well as mandates the person speak his/her truth. An understanding of perception as well as the ability to apply good communication skills is absolutely necessary for expression without accusation.   Honesty is crucial as the individuals seek to express facts as they understand them.

LISTEN TO UNDERSTAND – provides for unity of the heart. It means the person is open to new insight and encourages an awareness which prepares for compassionate response. It requires the person to be totally devoted to truly listening for meaning, rather than thinking of his/her answer as the other person speaks. It allows for each person to be heard, an extremely important component of the peacemaking process.

BRAINSTORM IDEAS – removes the barrier of limitations and allows for creative synergy to birth new concepts. It is a group process which liberates and causes new ways of thinking, acting, and being to be explored. It establishes an atmosphere where individuals are free to risk and become vulnerable activating their truest and best selves. The options constructed through brainstorming often produce win/win scenarios.

PICK A SOLUTION – evaluates and assesses the needs and opportunities of each option and formulates a conclusion. It considers the facts and opinions as well as the consequences of each choice. It defines the problem, honors the participants, takes the options into account, and makes a just and fair decision. It defines an action which is believed will be beneficial to the problem.

MAKE A PLAN. GO FOR IT! – tests the effectiveness of the decision. It takes the intentions from a premise and moves them into the realm of action. Success here is defined as the effort. If this particular conclusion wasn't quite right, the participants simply reevaluate their brainstorming ideas, choose another response, and apply it to the situation.

You can spend your time walking circles around
the abyss, or you can build a bridge over it.
~ Author unknown

The bridge is truly representative of the interpersonal peace process because it requires both sides to work together to come to a resolution. Unless each is a willing participant, all the overcompensating and "fixing" in the world won't help. It is simply one area where cooperation is necessary. When one side chooses to hold on to resentment, or a power base of bullying, or any other destructive behavior, the peacemaker needs to accept this decision and move on. When there is a true intention and desire to get along combined with knowledge and practice of a skill base, this ideal is absolutely possible!

You can't do it alone!

"Bridges to Understanding" has been included in this text to provide a cohesiveness to the individual lessons. The actual bridge, in a travel size, and complete instructions are available at www.celebratingpeace.com. Click on the bridge word or picture. This design is protected by international law. Please do not make your own. The money generated through the sale of this bridge goes to give peace resources away to those who cannot afford them and to create new resources such as this book.

LET THE DUST SETTLE

Depending on the personalities engaged in a disagreement, it may be wise to take some time apart from each other to regain composure before the issues can be worked out in a peaceful way. This work is the responsibility of the individual who may not have yet gained the ability to express his/her feelings through productive means. The individual must recognize his/her personal need, and take the necessary steps of emotional release. While it is true there are no "good" or "bad" emotions, it is equally true there are healthy and unhealthy ways to express those emotions. Acting out in a way which hurts the individual, others, or property is not a constructive way to relieve volatile emotions. Many people use the intensity of feelings as an excuse for poor behavior. Each person is always responsible for their own actions. Taking time to regain presence of mind so the peace process can be enhanced is sometimes a helpful step in preventing additional damage and escalation of the problem to a deeper level. This time of settling is never an excuse for simply avoiding the other person and leaving the issue unresolved.

~ MATERIALS ~

- empty baby food or other small jar
- water
- glitter
- small plastic figurine
- watertight adhesive
  (found in a hardware store)
- food coloring
  (very messy and stains clothing)

Use the adhesive to attach the figurine to the inside of the jar lid. Allow the adhesive to dry. Fill the jar with water and add a drop of food coloring if desired. Add glitter to the water. Apply adhesive to the inside of the jar lid and twist it onto the jar. Allow the jar to remain upright until the adhesive has had the required amount of drying time so the jar is sealed. Play with the "snow globe" by shaking the jar and watching the glitter dance as it falls to the bottom.

Relate the settling of the glitter to the calmness which needs to occur within the individual before peaceful conflict resolution can begin. Name and discuss techniques which are beneficial in helping people to be even-tempered. Remember to preserve the goal of healthy expression.

CALM, COOL & COLLECTED

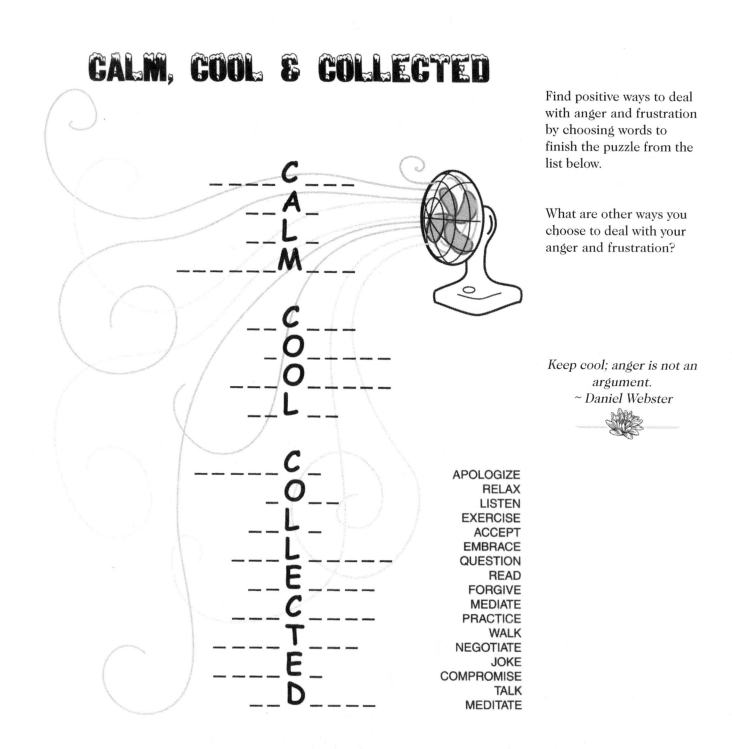

Find positive ways to deal with anger and frustration by choosing words to finish the puzzle from the list below.

What are other ways you choose to deal with your anger and frustration?

Keep cool; anger is not an argument.
~ Daniel Webster

APOLOGIZE
RELAX
LISTEN
EXERCISE
ACCEPT
EMBRACE
QUESTION
READ
FORGIVE
MEDIATE
PRACTICE
WALK
NEGOTIATE
JOKE
COMPROMISE
TALK
MEDITATE

A BRAINSTORM

Synergy is a process where the product is greater than the sum of the parts.

A brainstorm is a synergistic group process which frees all participants to think outside their normal strategies and create new outcomes. The technique stimulates fresh thoughts which give a wider range of options when considering a course of action.

In order for brainstorming to be effective, the spontaneity must not be inhibited by the fear of judgement. Brainstorming is not the time for analyzation or assessment of any type. It sometimes appears to be in disarray, but out of the chaos wonderful new approaches and options are born.

The code which must be enforced in brainstorming is - **no option will be harmful to self, others or property.**

~ MATERIALS ~
- marker
- large paper
- copies of page 100

Practice brainstorming. Enlarge the picture on page 100 for your canvas or write the ideas on a large piece of paper. Everyone needs to see what the ideas are as they are contributed. The person writing down the concepts must be someone who can write fast as sometimes the ideas come very quickly. There is a rhythm to productive brainstorming. The participants need to be encouraged to say whatever idea pops into their head as soon as they think of it. One idea will prompt a similar concept or may take the focus in an entirely new direction. As the guide, present the problem or item for consideration. Reinforce there are no dumb ideas continually. Record the thoughts as quickly as possible. Don't let brainstorming continue too long. When the energy has left the process and ideas are slower to materialize, end the exercise. People should feel energized and amazed at the options they have created rather than depleted of all creativity.

Use the following suggestions to practice the technique of brainstorming -

- Why can't the bird fly?
- Each person wants to use the same pencil, what should they do?
- Why can't someone see a flower?

Brainstorming, like any other skill, takes time and practice to develop. Rehearse as a group on several different occasions. Distribute copies of page 100 so individuals can use the skill in their daily life to provide more options for personal decisions.

SHARE YOUR THOUGHTS ...

- Describe how brainstorming would be helpful when two people are very sure they are each "right."
- Explain some of the benefits of including more people in a decision.

SWIRLING COLORS

Serendipity is when good things are discovered by accident. It is a joyful surprise which is encountered rather than planned for. It communicates the spontaneous nature of the lifeforce and the mystery of the universe. The final outcome cannot always be predicted, there are happy developments along the journey. What a wonderful context in which to enjoy life!

~ MATERIALS ~

- shallow dish
- warm whole milk
- dish soap
- food coloring

Show all the ingredients to the peacemakers and ask them to predict what would happen if all the ingredients were mixed together. Pour the warm milk into the pie plate. Add a few drops of each food coloring at various places in the milk. Add a few drops of dishwashing liquid to the mixture. (The effect is a bubbling, swirling canvas of color. The soap molecules attach to the milk's fat and water molecules giving the mixture a life of its own.) The group may want to repeat the process experimenting with a variety of color combinations.

SHARE YOUR THOUGHTS...

- If you were surprised by what happened when all the ingredients were mixed together, describe what surprised you.
- Has there been a time in your life when you were surprised by something good you did not anticipate? Please share.
- How can you help create joyful surprises for other people?

AFRICAN PROVERB

THE TREE REMEMBERS, THE AX FORGETS.

This African proverb demonstrates the devastation which can occur when relationships are in turmoil.

There is no way to overestimate the value of the simple words, "I'm sorry." They can be an incredible healing balm. They are interpreted as sincere when given freely and when the words which follow describe a behavior or feeling. (*e.g.,* "I'm sorry I yelled," or "I'm sorry you were hurt.") Used in this way, they convey that the speaker acknowledges the pain of another and wishes things were different.

If these simple words are used with any qualifiers though, "I'm sorry, if...," or given under duress such as when a parent insists a child apologize to another or when the person is afraid they will get caught, they are robbed of their sincerity, depth of intention, and the purity of meaning.

I'm sorry. It doesn't get any simpler, yet the need to speak the words as well as hear them is tremendous.

WIPE THE SLATE CLEAN

Forgiveness is a personal choice which allows the individual to quit dwelling within a hurtful situation and put his/her energy into new places. It frees the mind to move from dwelling in a "what if" mode to one of "what next?" The process doesn't demand the incident be forgotten, but merely clears the way for a new or different link. It is about acceptance, not approval. It does not sanction the offending behavior. The act of forgiveness is as much a gift to the individual doing the forgiving as it is for the relationship.

~ MATERIALS ~

· cornstarch
· spoon
· sugar
· water
· measuring cups

· food coloring
· clear packing tape
· plastic sandwich bags with top seal
· pan
· heat source

Advance preparation – Mix the following ingredients and cook over medium heat until thick: 1 cup cornstarch, 1/3 cup sugar, 4 cups water. Let the mixture cool to room temperature.

Assist the peacemakers in assembling their "slate." Place the substance into plastic bags which seal shut at the top. Add a few drops of food coloring into the bag and seal it. Knead (squish around) to distribute the color thoroughly. Reinforce the seal with clear wide packing tape. The amount of substance in the bag is determined by the size of the bag. When placed flat on the table, the substance should be approximately 1/4 inch thick with room to be displaced slightly when the slate is used.

The bag, which has now become a slate, is placed on a flat surface. Use a finger to draw designs into the slate. When a new picture is desired, no problem, simply redistribute the slate's contents by rubbing the palm over the bag.

As the fun is occurring, make sure the peacemakers understand that fixing a real hurt is not as easy as simply wiping this slate clean.

Forgiveness is the fragrance the violet
sheds on the heel that has crushed it.
~ Mark Twain

SHARE YOUR THOUGHTS ...

• Describe what it means to forgive someone.
• How do you go forward after a hurt and trust someone again?

PEACE TREE

In many different cultures, a tree is a symbol of peace. An olive branch is recognized across the globe as a peace emblem. Likewise, the so ɗ tree brings expression of the peace concept to the people in central Africa, as does the banyan tree to the people of East India. Native Americans also based meaning and tradition on indigenous trees. The Iroquois Indians had a rite of actually burying their weapons in the ground under a tree and then assigning guardian responsibility to an eagle so their enemies would not come to the defenseless people and make war.

Reconciliation is a process which demands both sides in the conflict work together to resolve the issue. It is a give and take between equals where each puts the other's needs ahead of his/her own. It embraces all dimensions of the individual. Reconciliation is a healing and bonding endeavor and has the potential to empower vital commitment to the pursuit of peace.

~ MATERIALS ~

- pencils
- small note cards or paper
- peace tree tapestry
- small dove puppet or paper likeness

The peace tree tapestry can be made very elaborately as pictured – a quilt of an olive tree complete with olives in different stages of ripeness, signifying color difference – or as a bulletin board made of paper. One small "branch" must be removable and replaceable and the ground underneath the tree needs to contain "pockets."

Ask the peacemakers to think of the "weapons" they use. A good way to create understanding of the concept is to ask, "What are the things you do which are hurtful." Talk about hurtful things – actions or words, and helpful things.

The peacemakers will then "dig" deep within themselves to identify the "weapons," hurtful things they personally use. Each person will then write down on the note card his/her weapon and "bury" it by placing it in a pocket found in the dirt.

The peacemakers will then take turns placing the detachable olive branch in the dove's mouth and handing it out to a friend while at the same time announcing the gift of peace they commit to share together.

* It is especially important to point out that no one is hiding the weapon, but rather identifying it, accepting it as part of the self, and then choosing not to use it against others. Just as the tree takes nutrients from the soil, a reconciled relationship grows stronger from this process of honest sharing.

TORN APART

No matter what the intention or skill level of people, hurt is going to occur. When it does, there is a possibility for people to mend the relationship in such a way where the restored relationship is actually stronger than the original bond. This of course is not an excuse to be careless and do damage to one another, but rather an opportunity for both parties go through the necessary steps where each feels understood, honored, and an enriched commitment to peacemaking is insured.

Restitution is a justice issue. It is accomplished through a reconciliatory process. Unlike forgiveness, reconciliation is not one sided, it can only occur when both sides agree to work on the problem and may involve the exchange of goods to correct the inequity.

~ MATERIALS ~
- construction paper
- glue
- markers or crayons

Hand out construction paper to the peacemakers. Ask them to use their imagination to turn tiny bits of paper into a larger design. (This is called a mosaic.) Each person will rip the paper to make the smaller pieces used in the design. As they progress, talk about what the ripping is doing to the piece of paper. The sound will add to the correlation between the art project they are participating in and the hurt that is caused when relationships are torn apart, or the peace is broken.

Next use a full sheet of the construction paper as the canvas and glue the pieces of ripped paper onto the canvas to create a picture.

SHARE YOUR THOUGHTS...

- Tell about a time when you hurt someone else. What did you do to fix the friendship?
- Name some things two people could do when they are mad at each other which would help fix, or act like glue, so the people will be friends again.
- Name some things that would not be helpful for people to do when there is a break in their friendship.

WHEN PROBLEMS CONTINUE

There are times when the ideals expressed in this book are not possible because both sides are not willing to work together to solve the problem. Sometimes people may say they want to work things out, but their motivations and actions are not based on what is best for everyone. They want things their way without respect for others' thoughts, feelings and needs.

All people exhibit different behaviors depending on the situation. At some point though, a prominent behavioral style emerges through a pattern of repeated use. It is important to understand these styles so that appropriate responses can be developed.

Assertive people are secure in their own sense of self and respect, support, and defend the rights of others. They are selfless in nature, but also practice good self care and do not feel guilty about this energizing time. They are very effective in their ability to get things accomplished. The methods they use are based in mutual respect and trust. Assertive people value multiple opinions and the individuality of others. They view each person as important and equal. They are effective in their leadership, creating a collaborative climate which expresses vision, kindness, and encouragement. Assertive people's identities are based not in simply what they do, but in who they are at their essence.

Non-assertive people confuse the concept of being liked with that of being respected. They value the idea of people liking them to such an extent that they engage in self-limiting attitudes and behaviors. Eventually the submissive pattern of behavior is internalized to such an extent that they become extremely self-conscious and fearful of realizing their full potential. Their identity is determined by what others think of them. This fear translates into a lack of action. Non-assertive people allow themselves to be dominated by others because they begin to believe they are inferior to others.

Aggressive people may appear self-confident, but this demeanor is really an arrogance based upon low self-esteem. They force and draw attention to their own prominence as part of the mask of insecurity and lack of self-acceptance. Ego and good self-esteem are inversely proportional. The more extravagant the flaunting and boasting of abilities, the weaker the individual is in his/her perception of self and worth. Likewise, the stronger and healthier the sense of self, the less a person needs external gratification. Aggressive people make their decisions through autocratic procedures. They demand rather than request, push their own agenda, and demean those who disagree. These actions are justified because they have an imperial view of the world where their own rights are superior to others.

Aggressive people quite commonly are educated in the most current jargon of teamwork, representing and promoting themselves as something they are not. Instead, their methodology represses truth, dominates opportunities, and oppresses others' giftedness. Their very identity is based upon who they have power over. Commonly, aggressive people are not held accountable for their behavior and in fact flourish in society because they do get things done. They make things happen. The problem is, the ends do not justify the means. It is NEVER acceptable for anyone to usurp the rights of another individual.

Bullying is an early form of aggressive behavior. Like all behaviors, it is learned at home, and if not confronted can degenerate into other forms of violence. When a person chooses to behave in an aggressive manner, they are a perpetrator, they harm others and create victims. To deny the label minimizes the actions, negates the patterns of behavior, and contributes to the dysfunction. The damage is a reality, the confrontation of the actions must also be real.

A person who has chosen the path of the perpetrator is one who has become expert in the behavior which perpetuates the ability to create more harm. The world revolves around his/her axis and, therefore, all the subsequent necessary actions are sanctified. S/he redefines truth, reconstructs history to his/her own benefit, attacks the victim's credibility, and rewards those who enable the aggressive behavior.

The prevailing cultural norm toward aggressive actions is not a healthy attitude. A common symptomatic response is a tendency to blame the victim. The pull not to get involved is based upon the fear of becoming one of the perpetrator's victims, as well as intuitively understanding the responsibilities advocacy requires. The avoidance mechanism can be so strong that it manifests itself by denying the offense even occurred or by battering the victim with the dirge of "forgive and forget." This phrase has nothing to do with the actual forgiving process, but rather is an effort by the third party to ignore the problem. Another factor in refusing to engage in justice making is a "false compassion" syndrome where the person focuses on the "goodness" of the perpetrator. It does not matter if perpetrators are "good people at heart" or not, they have done harm through their choices and must be held accountable for their actions. A witness or third party cannot remain morally neutral. There is a choice to be made. The choice is simple, denying reality exacerbates the problem, assertive action begins the justice process and therefore the healing.

A new understanding of effective approaches and standards based upon civility need to be integrated within a social context. Confrontation is not the same as combativeness. Confrontation is an assertive action, combativeness is an aggressive one. To confront simply means to seek truth. It is a healthy way for people to deal with aggressive behaviors. In order for justice and healing to occur, everyone must do one simple thing – speak their truth. There is no greater power. It is simple, but it is not easy. We need a zone of safety where harm is acknowledged, accountability and consequences are enforced, and restitution is applied including exonerating the victim. This reconciliatory process is beneficial to both the victim and the perpetrator. It is an expression of true compassion because when the perpetrator is held accountable, s/he is forced to face his/her own demons. With this inner personal work comes the opportunity to reclaim his/her dreams, to abandon his/her regrets and jealousies, and to stop venting in inappropriate and hurtful ways.

PEACE FOR EVERYONE

Peace for Everyone focuses on the concepts of justice, compassionate action, equality, and group empowerment.

The development of a social consciousness has been demonstrated to me in remarkable terms by my daughter, Kristen. Her first act of selfless devotion happened when she was three years old. Her dance teacher told her there were children in the world who wouldn't be getting Christmas presents. Immediately when she got home, Kristen got her favorite toy, her treasured pickup truck, and began wrapping it so she could give it to someone else. Throughout her life, she has been engaged in the service of life and has incorporated this active participation into her personal philosophy. During her freshman year of high school her teacher, Mr. Brown, was talking to the class about the Holocaust. He was emphasizing the fact that the evil prospered because the good people were afraid and did nothing. He was reflective and honest and told the students that if he would have been born in that time and space he too might have simply looked out for himself in order to make it through the atrocities alive. He then turned to Kristen and said, "You would have been dead in the first fifteen minutes." At first Kristen didn't understand what a huge compliment he had given her. There was no doubt in his mind that she, regardless of the consequences, would have stood up for justice. Kristen understands compassionate action and advocacy, she engages in good causes and views life through a spirit of generosity.

GOLDEN QUESTION

No one knows exactly when character is formed or precisely what determines the overall way in which an individual interprets life's experiences. Increasingly, brain research shows these traits developing earlier than anyone has ever anticipated. Empathy is the ability to understand what another person is feeling. It is different than sympathy or compassion in that it is actually based on an experiential understanding level. A person can empathize with someone when they liken the other person's experience to one of his/her own which share similarities.

A 16-month-old child was with her grandma. Her mother had taught her sign language to help her communicate before she had the ability to articulate many words. The child kept saying and signing that she wanted to go talk to her "Bompa," grandpa, on the phone. The grandma told the child that he was sick and they couldn't talk to him, but when he was better they could see him. The child was not comprehending so the grandma used the sign for grandpa and pain. Immediately the little girl furled her brow in an empathetic gesture and began to express a clearly sincere and caring statement of concern even though it was not discernable to adult ears.

People from all over the world believe through their faith structures in what is sometimes called "The Golden Rule." Research and talk about the different interpretations of the principle as found on page 110.

This "Golden Rule" can be turned into a "Golden Question." Make large gold question marks which can be hung all over asking the question, "Is this how you'd like to be treated?" It's amazing the change in behavior that occurs when this simple visual reminder is present. Soon, the question becomes an internal thought process which changes the "normal" way an individual approaches life.

Please note, when people are very damaged they will often claim they don't care how they are treated, so they will treat everyone else however they want to. Sometimes it is helpful to spend concentrated time identifying people they do care about and who they do want treated in a kind and nice way. Behavior agreements can then be based on how they want their chosen people treated. Obviously, more extensive help is needed through professionals to help this type of broken person learn to value him/herself.

The practice of empathy is a universal principle expressed by all major religions. It is used as a way of teaching a behavior which demonstrates value and respect through the ability to recognize the similar feelings and needs of all people. Empathy creates a sense of oneness.

Hinduism
"This is the sum of duty: do naught to others which if done to thee would cause thee pain."
The Mahabharata

Judaism
"What is hateful to you, do not to your fellow man. That is the entire law, all the rest is commentary."
The Talmud

Buddhism
"Hurt not others with that which pains yourself."
Udana - Varqa

Christianity
"Do unto others as you would have them do unto you."
The Book of Matthew

Islam
"No one of you is a believer until he desires for his brother that which he desires for himself."
Hadith

SHARE YOUR THOUGHTS ...

- Talk about how empathy can help solve problems.
- What do you think the world would look like if all people practiced empathy?
- Name specific things your group can do to demonstrate empathy.

CONNECTING WITH THE HEART

Compassion is tenderness, a depth of understanding so penetrating the person shares the feelings of another being. Compassion provides insight into the actions and perspectives of another person and responds with forgiveness, love, and kindness. It is a healing energy within each person which motivates service and encourages a sense of wonder in the beauty of humankind. It softens and removes the boundaries of fear and hate, creating a climate of acceptance and mutual respect.

~ MATERIALS ~
- pencils
- copies of this page

As long as there is one compassionate woman, the contagion may spread and the scene is not desolate.
~ E.B. White

Compassion is nurtured through building relationships. Find peacemakers who fit the description for each square. Ask them to sign their name in the square. If possible, you'll need to find a different person for each square.

Someone whose favorite sandwich is the same as yours	Someone who has the same number of brothers and sisters as you	Someone who has the same color of eyes as you	Someone who likes to play soccer	Someone whose name begins with the same letter as yours
Someone who plays a musical instrument	Someone who was born the same month as you	Someone who likes to read	Someone who is wearing the same color of socks as you	Someone who has a pet

SHARE ideas about the importance of people getting to know one another. How does compassion help people better understand each other? How can we become more compassionate people?

JUST LIKE ME

People of all cultures celebrate life's journey through rituals. The rite may be to honor the birth of a baby, as a marriage sacrament, or to observe a special holiday. During these times, traditional food, games, songs, and clothing may be part of the celebration. They are times to remember heritage, connect in relationships, and offer gratitude for the gift of life.

This panel was made for the first PeaceMobile (information about PeaceMobile is found on page 129). It is a quilt where the traditional dress of many cultures is shown. It provides the opportunity for people to see themselves as "foreign," in another person's "skin,"as participants peek through the holes and look at their reflection in a full-length

mirror. The people looking through the panel in this picture are seeing themselves differently than they normally look. Literally, when they take a step back the barrier is removed and the people see one another as "Just Like Me." The outer appearance may be quite different, but inside we are all people who love, and laugh, and sing, and cry, and celebrate, and live!

Make your own "Just Like Me" banner, as shown in the illustration on this page. An elaborate quilt can be made or a more simple version can be created from a sheet or even a large roll of paper. Research the traditional dress of people around the world and find a word or two indigenous to the culture. Remember to leave enough room to place your face through the hole. And, don't forget the full-length mirror held so each may see him/herself as a person from a different culture.

(information about PeaceMobile is found on page 129)

SHARE YOUR THOUGHTS...

• What are some differences which make people unique?
• What are some ways that all people are the same?
• How can we help others see that we can unite as one, and it doesn't mean we have to be the same?

CUSTOMS & TRADITIONS

Cultural differences are traits or characteristics which are passed from generation to generation. They are what is defined as normal for a particular place or people. Many cultural aspects are not taught verbally, they are simply part of the daily fabric of life; therefore, people aren't even aware of some of the nuances. This lack of awareness may cause confusion in interactions between diverse people.

~ MATERIALS ~

- pencils
- paper
- tape measure
- scissors

Instruct the peacemakers to trace around their feet, cut out the tracing, and write their name on it. Next have one person stand in a fixed position while everyone else takes turns walking up to that person to start a conversation. This is something that is not calculated beforehand, simply done as the person will stop at their "natural" distance to talk to the other person. Place the paper feet down at this ideal distance. After everyone has had a chance, mark the following distances:

6 1/4 inches - Middle East
18 3/4 inches - Latin America and Southern Europe
28 inches - North America and Africa
45 inches - Asia
63 inches - Germany and Northern Europe

The distances represent the conversational space traditional to the culture within the geographic area. The space varies because the method of greeting which is the most usual for the culture is the determining factor in conversational distance, *e.g.*, a handshake, a bow, a kiss on the cheek. Other communication subtleties which vary between cultures are, whether to look each other in the eye while speaking, and whether or not to respond with a nod or comment when spoken to.

SHARE YOUR THOUGHTS ...

- How can cultural differences cause misunderstanding between people?
- What can be done to respect each other's culture and produce fewer misunderstandings?

CONNECTING

The call of peacemaking challenges humanity to move beyond tolerance to acceptance. It is an impassioned plea undergirding the rights, dignity, and equality of all. How a person handles diversity depends largely upon how comfortable they are within themselves. The connecting fiber of the still small voice within calls each individual to the compassion of interdependent relationships.

~ MATERIALS~
- popsicle sticks or twigs
- yarn in many colors
- scissors

Position two popsicle sticks as shown and secure them by wrapping the yarn diagonally around the two several times.

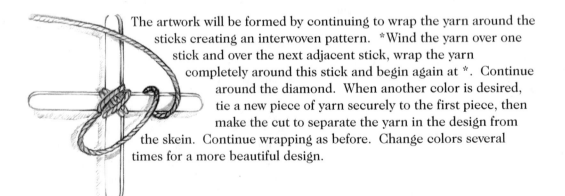

The artwork will be formed by continuing to wrap the yarn around the sticks creating an interwoven pattern. *Wind the yarn over one stick and over the next adjacent stick, wrap the yarn completely around this stick and begin again at *. Continue around the diamond. When another color is desired, tie a new piece of yarn securely to the first piece, then make the cut to separate the yarn in the design from the skein. Continue wrapping as before. Change colors several times for a more beautiful design.

While creating the design, talk about how our lives are connected and interwoven with each other and the benefits this bonding creates for each person.

BIAS

A bias is an unjust policy or action based on a preconceived judgement about a person or groups of persons. The determination is nonobjective and many times is based upon external factors such as skin color or a speech dialect. Bias prevents fairness from occurring as it is rooted in stereotypes and discrimination. It creates profiling, denies equal rights to all, and promotes inequality.

~ MATERIALS ~
- a sandwich cookie with a creme center
- table knife
- plate
- white toothpaste
- trash can

I have a dream that my four little children will one day live in a nation where they will not be judged by the color of their skin but by the content of their character. I have a dream today!
~ Dr. Martin Luther King, Jr.

Carefully open the cookie and remove the creme filling. Put a large dab of toothpaste inside the cookie. Do this with several cookies and arrange them attractively on the plate.

When the peacemakers bite into the cookies, they will be extremely surprised at the resulting taste. Talk about the phrase "You can't judge a book by its cover."

Share in the following definitions of stereotype, prejudice and discrimination.

STEREOTYPE
Thinking everyone in a group is the same.
NOT KEEPING SPECIAL

PREJUDICE
Unfair judgement of others because of stereotypes. Making a decision on whether you like someone or not before you get to know them.
UNFAIR DECISIONS

DISCRIMINATION
People's actions are based on their stereotypes and prejudices. Not respecting the rights of other people because they are different than you.
ACTING UNKIND

SHARE experiences about bias. Talk about how you can help people see the wonder of each special person.

BELONGING

From a very young age, children are taught to differentiate between objects in a group. Items which share similarities are grouped together. The object which is different is labeled as "not belonging." This categorization continues into other areas of life and "different" is interpreted as separate rather than part of an inclusive whole. The challenge is to view diversity as a significant strength and very much belonging to the group.

The mobius is a paradox, a seemingly impossible phenomenon. It is a three-dimensional object which only has a single side. Rather than having separate sides and edges, there is only one side and one edge; a unity which demonstrates the interconnectedness of all people. Use the mobius to demonstrate how humanity can truly be "on the same side."

~ MATERIALS ~
- scissors
- tape
- paper
- pencil

Ask each peacemaker to cut a strip of paper about 11 inches long by 3 inches wide. On each side, draw a dotted line lengthwise down the middle of the paper. Twist the strip a half turn so the front of the paper meets the back and anchor it together with tape. (See illustration.) Using the scissors, cut along the dotted line. The result of this cut is not two separate circles, but rather one large unending strip. * Once again, cut the strip in half lengthwise all the way around. The result this time is two united circles.

After the first cut is completed, engage in a discussion of seeing the value in differences (diversity) and the concept of unity – there is no need to take sides because there truly is only one side and we are all on it together.

After the second cut is completed, SHARE in a discussion of the definition of community and how each life is interconnected.

*Though I am different from you, we were
born involved in one another.
~ T'ao Chien*

UNDER MY THUMB

Oppression is a type of injustice which keeps people from reaching their potential. It is cruel. Its goal is to dominate another human being. Oppression can take many forms and runs the gamut from the extreme persecution of ethnic groups of people to the more subtle coercion which occurs in "developed" societies. Oppression is an external force which creates hardship and eventually can undermine the inner confidence of the victim.

A person who uses oppression as a weapon is one who is insecure about him/herself and needs to overpower another in order to feel important. Because of this imbalance, the perpetrator attempts to conquer, to make others' giftedness cease and desist so the perpetrator will feel elevated.

Ask a large adult to sit in a chair with his/her feet flat on the floor and hands on his/her lap. Ask a child, who when standing is slightly taller than the sitting adult, to participate. The child will stand directly in front of the adult and place one thumb on the middle of the adult's upper forehead. Using only his/her thumb, the child will press gently but firmly down and back on the adult's forehead. The adult will attempt to stand up. As long as the child keeps the pressure on the forehead with the thumb, the adult will be unable to rise up.

In this example, a much smaller force is restraining or holding down a much larger strength simply by applying pressure in the right place. Oppression is like that. It holds people back by making them doubt their own internal power. Another interesting point is the perpetrator, is also trapped because if they were to move forward, they would lose the hold on the other individual.

Use this physical demonstration to introduce the abstract concept of oppression.

• Research and explore how oppressed people refused to see themselves as victims and stood up in nonviolent ways to their oppressors. Discuss the impact these movements have had on society.

• List instances where subtle forms of oppression occurs. What can be done about these "minor" abuses? Is anything "minor" if you are the one being taunted or mistreated?

• What can you do to help people to understand that any type of domination is not a peaceful behavior? When will you start?

Nearly all men can stand
adversity, but if you want to test a
man's character, give him power.
~ Abraham Lincoln

MINE!

Equity is a declaration of justice. It is a right where the privilege of expression is often held hostage. Equity is impartial fairness. It is a concept which is valuable in the minds of many people, but when it comes time for the application, those of advantage suddenly experience greed and an unwillingness to give up any leverage of power, possessions, or opportunities. Equity is equal rights and opportunities; it does not mean everyone has the same thing, but rather that everyone has their distinctive needs met.

A very simple way to illustrate the fairness aspect of equity is to take a piece of cake. Whoever chooses to cut the cake into two pieces must allow the other person to choose the slice they want.

Make copies of page 119. Using a different color for each group, color the jelly beans as directed.

1. On one page, use 4 different colors and make 57 jelly beans one color, 21 another color, 14 a third color, and the 8 remaining beans the fourth color. (It's more effective if each color is mixed throughout the jar.)

2. On a separate page, using 2 different colors, make 52 jelly beans one color and 48 the other color.

3. Using a third page and two colors, make 70 jelly beans one color and 30 the other color.

4. Use two pages together and one color. On one page color 6 jelly beans and on the second page color 60 jelly beans.

FROM JELLY BEANS TO HUMAN BEINGS

In example number one the world's population is represented by percentages in terms of distribution of people on land mass; the 57 are Asian, the 21 are European, the 14 are North and South American, and the 8 are African.

Example number 2 represents percentages of the world's population by gender, 52 being female, 48 male.

Example number 3 represents percentages of the world's population according to color, 70 are nonwhite, 30 are white. This jar is also representative of illiteracy (70) and literacy (30).

The last example represents the percentage of the world's population according to wealth. The 6 in the first jar have the 60 in the second jar. All six are from the United States.

*Ratios attributed to Stanford University

SHARE YOUR THOUGHTS...

• If anything surprised you during this exercise, please describe what it was.
• Discuss the unfairness represented as it relates to wealth, power, and opportunity.
• In the last example, what would be a fair distribution? If a real jar of jelly beans was brought into the room and given to one person, how equitably would that person choose to distribute them if the choice was entirely his/hers?

The good we secure for ourselves is precarious
and uncertain, until it is secured for all of us
and incorporated into our common life.
~ Jane Addams

THE HUMAN RACE

A team is supposed to be a group of people who are on the same side working for a common purpose. Yet, many times, teams who are united in force against others are also in competition within themselves to see who is "better than" the other players. Competition can be an incredibly motivating tool, but simultaneously creates a friction and distance between people. A change in mindset to a peace behavior facilitates a win/win environment which benefits all participants.

~ MATERIALS ~
- crepe paper streamer
- stop watch

This is an activity best done outside. Instruct the peacemakers to gather in one place. Construct a finish line a distance away from them. (The finish line is created by two people holding a long section of crepe paper streamer between them.) The peacemakers will then need to work together as a group to race as fast as they can to the finish line. The thing different about this race though is no one may touch the finish line until everyone reaches it. Everyone must go through the streamer at the finish line at the exact same moment or the time does not count. Repeat several times to see if the peacemakers can lessen the time it takes to reach the finish line. (It may take several times before individuals stop competing to reach the finish line first and begin acting as a group.) Hopefully, they will begin working together and thinking collaboratively to come up with a solution possibly like the one pictured here.

Another fun activity which challenges the competitive norm is cooperative musical chairs. Each time the music stops, a chair is removed, but all players stay. Everyone must sit down (not on the floor) whenever the music stops. The result is people gently sitting on each other's laps. When there is no chair left, the peacemakers will really have to think creatively to make a circle where everyone sits in unison on another person's lap.

SHARE together in the behavior observed during the activity. Identify the actions which were helpful to the group process and those which were not helpful. Discuss ways a group can act in respectful ways to accomplish a goal.

IT TAKES A TEAM

Mutualism is a symbiotic relationship, an association between two entities, where each is dependent on the other and each share in the benefits resulting from the alliance. When people work together collaboratively, each person must fulfill the expectation of the relationship or everyone suffers. It is in the best interest of all concerned for the group to set aside their individual agendas and concentrate instead on the collective objective.

~ MATERIALS ~

- write-on wipe-off marker board or large pieces of paper
- marker

As a group, read the following situations out loud. Discuss how the goal of the group is affected by one person's actions. What are the options?

You and your friends decide to go camping overnight. When you arrive, you find pouring rain and realize no one brought the tents.

A quartet (4 people singing different parts) decides to sing a special song at your teacher's retirement party. One person doesn't learn his/her part and decides not to come to any of the practices.

Your class divides into small groups to complete a project. Everyone in each small group will receive the same grade. Most of the people in your group work hard to do their best on the project; two people don't care about the project and refuse to help.

Work together to brainstorm types of teams commonly found in daily life. Write the ideas on the marker board. Examples might be – school band, baseball team, science club, etc.

Identify the goal of each team, why cooperation is important, as well as how they work together to accomplish the goal.

Next, think of several issues which seem too large for one person to make a difference (*e.g.*, hunger, illiteracy, etc.). Describe a goal to help the situation. Brainstorm an action plan identifying who needs to be on the team to accomplish this goal, how the team will work, and why cooperation is important.

WHAT SHALL WE DO?

When a group of people willingly join together to solve a problem, they enter into a creative process which liberates new possibilities and outcomes. The combination of brainstorming to tap into the collective intelligence, evaluation to choose the best solution, and establishing an implementation strategy maximizes the chance for success. In this way, the most effective outcome is realized to bless the group.

TOUCH THE BALL

~ MATERIALS ~
- small ball
- stop watch

The goal of this activity is for the ball to touch the hands of all the peacemakers in the shortest amount of time as possible. They may try as many different options as they can think of to get the best time.

(Common problem solving methods are: Going from tossing the ball to standing close to each other and handing the ball around a circle. Standing in a circle with one person holding the ball and running around the circle. One person holds the ball in the center of a circle and everyone steps in at the same time and touches the ball in unison.)

BRIDGES OF COOPERATION

~ MATERIALS ~
- gumdrops & toothpicks
or
- large marshmallows and spaghetti

Ask the peacemakers to divide into small groups. Using gumdrops and toothpicks OR marshmallows and uncooked spaghetti, work together to build a bridge. How long can you make the bridge before it collapses? How tall can it be?

SHARE YOUR THOUGHTS...

- Was your first idea the one that was most effective? Why or why not?
- What helped the group the most in finding a solution?

TOGETHER WE WILL....

Group interaction helps determine values, attitudes, and behaviors. When individuals make the choice to stand together, new opportunities are discovered which wouldn't have been possible when individuals act alone. It is a philosophy, a civility, which sanctions "power with" rather than "power over." Every person has the ability to choose what context they are contributing to the community. The choice is to contribute from the position of respect or neglect, understanding that all will experience the consequences of the decision.

ALL TANGLED UP

~ MATERIALS ~
• Scarf or hanky

Ask the peacemakers to form a circle. Each person holds onto the end of a hanky or scarf in one hand. With the other hand, each person grabs another person's scarf on the available end. The only requirement is the person whose scarf is selected cannot be directly next to the person who is doing the selection. (Everyone will be hanging on to a scarf in each hand.) When everyone is holding on to two scarves, there will be quite a tangled mess. Without letting go of either scarf, the peacemakers must work together to untangle themselves, ending once again in a circle.

THE GOAL

~ MATERIALS ~
• scissors
• tape
• marker
• paper

Using the marker and a piece of paper, write the word "Peace" on the piece of paper and hang it on the opposite side of the room. Instruct the peacemakers to divide into teams. Give each team a piece of paper, scissors, and tape. Each team will create something with their paper which will come as close to the center of "Peace" (hanging on the wall) as possible when thrown from across the room. The teams will need to use their group skills of brainstorming as well as the talents of the team members to accomplish this goal. (Hint: Most teams will make a variety of different paper airplanes. Thinking outside the box though, simply wadding the paper up and throwing it as a ball will probably be more accurate.) Each team will take their turns "aiming for peace."

SHARE YOUR THOUGHTS...

• How well did your group do in the cooperative process? Was everyone's ideas considered, etc.? Please explain.
• What could have made the process better ?
• In "The Goal" how could listening to each other and taking the time to plan help to create a more successful outcome?

BALANCING ACT

The ability to work jointly to accomplish a goal increases the chance for the outcome to be more effective and the experience more meaningful. The balance of affirming the giftedness of the individual and incorporating additional perspectives is accomplished through cooperation. The dynamics of group interaction requires the interpersonal peacemaking skills of effective communication and respectful behavior, even when in crisis, to be understood and practiced.

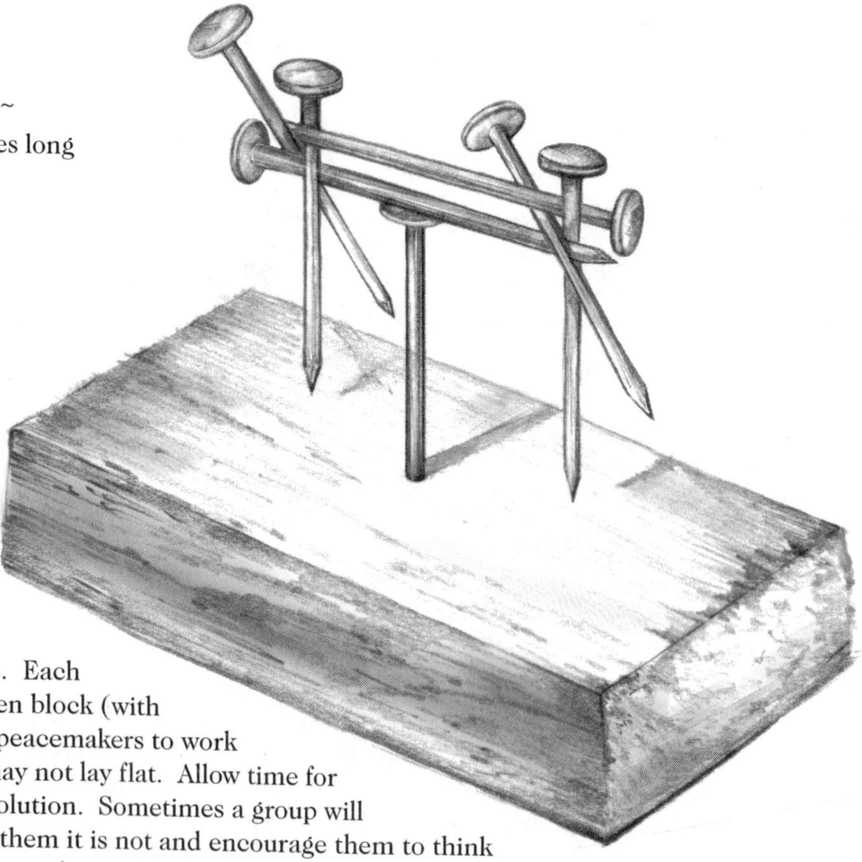

~ MATERIALS ~
- nails about 3 inches long
- hammer
- wooden block

In advance of the group activity, hammer one nail into the wooden block so it forms an upright support.

Ask the peacemakers to divide into teams. Each team will be given six nails and one wooden block (with one nail hammered into it). Instruct the peacemakers to work together to balance the nails. The nails may not lay flat. Allow time for the teams to work together to think of a solution. Sometimes a group will conclude it is an impossible task. Assure them it is not and encourage them to think creatively, promising to show them the answer later. (Shown here is one answer.)

SHARE together how each group worked together to accomplish something difficult. Point out what types of behaviors were respectful and what type made someone feel like his/her ideas weren't valuable. Talk of ways people can change their behavior in order to be a better representation of a peacemaker.

COMMON GOAL

When a group of people work together toward a common purpose, individuals can concentrate on developing and applying their unique gifts. Each person is free to be their truest and best self. Collaboration creates a culture of trust resulting in synergistic outcomes not previously thought possible. Collaboration is distinctly different than compromise. Compromise is often a system of negotiation which is based on "How little can I lose while gaining the most." Collaboration, however, is grounded by an abundance mentality where each side gives their very best, knowing and expecting there will be more than enough.

A mosaic is an image formed by uniting different colors and surfaces together to create a composite piece of art.

~ MATERIALS ~
- jelly beans
- peanut butter
- popsicle stick
  to spread the peanut butter
- copy of this page
- tape
- camera

Using a copy machine or overhead projector, enlarge the pattern until it is about 16 inches across and tape the separate pieces together to form a whole. Lay the pattern on a table. The peacemakers will need to wash their hands. They will use the peanut butter as the "glue" and the jelly beans as the tiles. Apply the peanut butter to one section at a time, then fill in that section with jelly beans. Work together to create a colorful mosaic.

When completed, take a picture of the peacemakers with their mosaic.

Next, just as the Buddhist monks sweep away their beautiful sand mandalas, disassemble and eat the mosaic reinforcing the idea that peace is not something you work on and then leave; it is something that needs the nurture of creating every day.

SHARE with each other and talk about how each jelly bean retains its own identity while contributing to something beautiful. List some things you do alone which may turn out better if you would unite and work with someone else.

WINGS OF KINDNESS

Kindness is peacemaking made real. It is an expression, a lifestyle, which manifests the generosity of spirit essential to conceive a new archetype. Kindness practiced on the personal level generates wellness, demonstrated in relationships bears mutuality, and offered to the planet protects the delicate balance.

The Kindness Campaign is an initiative where the people of the world have the opportunity to focus on what it means to be kind, to celebrate kindness! What a great way to build self-esteem, hold up mutual respect and increase the awareness of positive acts in everyday behavior. Helps have been created to assist in beginning and nurturing this successful effort of peace, justice, and goodwill. For more information, as well as resources, please visit www.celebratingpeace.com and click on the Kindness Campaign word or picture.

The Kindness Campaign's logo is a child's hand and a butterfly. An everyday object takes on symbolism based upon life experience. A child's hand and a butterfly are prevalent objects which share universal meanings in every culture. The butterfly represents freedom, beauty, energy, and spontaneity as it dances in flight. When kindness is as common as butterflies in a field of flowers on a summer day, there will be peace on earth.

The "Butterfly Effect" was the famous phrase discovered and chosen by meteorologist and mathematician Edward Lorenz to demonstrate that the tiniest of variables have tremendous consequences. Something as seemingly insignificant as the flap of one butterfly, when magnified over time and space, changes the entire weather pattern across the globe. Imagine then, what is capable of happening with an intentional focus on kindness!

~ MATERIALS ~
- washable markers
- coffee filters
- spray bottle
- water
- pipe cleaners
- old newspapers

Kind words can be short and easy to speak, but
their echoes are truly endless.
~ Mother Teresa

Use the markers and draw designs on the coffee filter. Place the filters on old newspapers and mist with water using the spray bottle. The colors will spread throughout the filter. When the filter has dried, pinch it together in the middle and fasten with a pipe cleaner. Twist the pipe cleaner together to form the body and antennae of a butterfly.

SHARE together in ways you can spread kindness. Focus on how one kind act can start a sequence or a chain reaction of goodness, peace, and love. Make a list of things you can do to be kind to yourself, your friends and family, other people, and the planet. Construct a plan on how you will support each other to start spreading kindness today.

MAKE YOUR MARK

Generosity is transforming to the person with the benevolent outlook as well as to the community s/he serves. The commitment necessary to fully invest in a cause makes life more worthwhile. When an individual refuses to look at the world from a consumer mentality expecting entitlement, but chooses instead a producer mentality which means engaging in the creative process, s/he releases the essence of who s/he is really created to be.

In this picture, the peacemaker is moving to leave an impression in the snow. This is commonly called a snow angel. Someone who lives where it never snows might automatically think s/he couldn't do the same thing and create an "angel." This person isn't thinking beyond what is normal and expected. What about a sand angel? This simple example tells us we must act to make a difference in the world. We need to think creatively and develop new ideas and ways of accomplishing good.

Amazing things have happened and the world has been changed for good because a single individual believed in his/her own greatness and began to act on those convictions.

Your work is to discover your world and then with all your heart give yourself to it.
~ Buddha

Research and find people who are "Peace heroes," individuals who had the courage to act to help bring peace in the world. Who were they? What were their causes? What were the goals? How did their actions help to create a more just society?

Create a "Peace hero" award and give it to people in your life when you see them making a positive difference.

GO LIGHT YOUR WORLD

Service learning is when people join together and work to make a positive difference. The key is active participation. They get involved in something beyond their own life and cooperate with others to help or create positive change. When people engage in this way, they discover new traits within their altruistic self, learn about others, and enlarge their sense of connectedness.

~ MATERIALS ~

- sliced bananas
- forks
- pineapple sections
- orange or apple sections
- maraschino cherries
- plates
- lettuce leaf

Many times people get discouraged about some of the world's problems and never do anything to help. They become overwhelmed before they even start. They can list a multitude of reasons why they can't, which when looked at objectively are really excuses. Perhaps one way to stop this "can't do" attitude is to quit thinking about how huge THE world is and concentrate efforts on YOUR world. If everyone would simply bring one ray of hope to his/her immediate world, what a difference it would make in the world!

Create a candle as shown by combining the fruit.

Sing "This Little Light of Mine," or another song together.

Better to light a candle than to curse the darkness.
~ Chinese proverb

SHARE together something you are passionate about, a cause you would like to work at. What's preventing you from doing good? How can you eliminate the obstacles and begin?

PEACEMOBILE

The PeaceMobile is a traveling children's museum which teaches the same positive life skills as this book – Peace for Me, Peace for Us, Peace for Everyone, Peace for the Planet. Embracing the enthusiasm, excitement, curiosity, and spontaneity of children, the PeaceMobile promotes peace through intergenerational play. Children and their families learn how to build peace through a fantastic array of interactive, hands-on activities and exhibits.

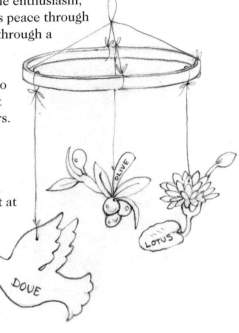

The PeaceMobile began in Nebraska when a group of volunteers decided to do something to enhance their community. In the first two years, this one effort touched the lives of 52,000 children and utilized the skills of 1,400 volunteers. Since that time, several other PeaceMobiles have been developed around the world. For more information about the PeaceMobile, go to www.celebratingpeace.com and click on the PeaceMobile word or picture.

The PeaceMobile, which goes to where the people are with fun exhibits, is not at all related to a peace mobile which will be constructed in this lesson.

A visual symbol takes something that is abstract, like peace, and links it with something that is physical and has meaning in daily life. Symbols are important not simply for the awareness they convey, but for the way in which they serve as reminders to practice the skills and express the values they represent.

~ MATERIALS ~

- scissors
- glue
- pencils
- string
- paper
- paper punch
- small ring such as embroidery hoop
- glitter and other decorative material
- research material

The young do not know enough to be prudent, and therefore they attempt the impossible and achieve it.
~ Pearl S. Buck

Ask the peacemakers to do research into what types of objects symbolize or represent peace to people around the world. Create a list of possibilities. (There are many other examples besides those illustrated here; deer, tree, lion & lamb, the hand with two fingers in the form of a "V," etc.) The peacemakers will then use the supplies to create their own peace mobile placing the images around the hoop as shown. Hang the mobile in a place where it will remind people to practice peaceful behavior.

Share together in the website www.celebratingpeace.com. Perhaps you'd like to join the global grassroots effort represented on the site. Or, maybe you'd like to contribute artwork to the Visions of Peace Art Collection. Talk together about ways you can share peace with others.

I WANT TO BE A PEACEMAKER

PEACE FOR THE PLANET

Peace for the planet links humankind in a respectful relationship with the earth and its inhabitants. I have intentionally made this section smaller because in order to truly appreciate other forms of life, you must be outside interacting with nature. To be a steward of the earth means you are concerned with its wellbeing not simply for the period of your lifetime, but for the sustainability of the entire life force well beyond the present.

Some of my most precious moments have been when I have been intentional about connecting with nature. Whether it was running through the Loess hills collecting "Easter flowers" as a child, dancing in the rain with my own children, or simply walking by myself contemplating the mysteries of life, I have felt such a sense of completeness simply being centered in the present moment.

A PEACE GARDEN

Peace gardens have been planted as a way to share peace with the community. The lotus blossom on the bottom corner of this book is a symbol of peace in and of itself; a plant whose roots are in the mud and muck and yet still reaches for the light to share its beauty. It is also a symbol of the peace process; not a destination, but a journey. (Flip the corner of the book in a rapid manner and animate the lotus as it goes from bud to flower to seed pod.) A flower has not accomplished its reason for being on the planet simply by blooming, it is only when it produces seed that it has fulfilled its mission. Humanity's purpose is also to contribute in a benevolent way to the earth and its inhabitants.

A peace garden can be anything you want it to be. Some examples are:
- A "cutting garden" where there are signs saying "Please DO pick the flowers."
- A labyrinth made up of grass and flowers.
- A beautiful place to sit and rest.
- A living monument to peace as in the case when the flowers are grouped by color to create an image. (A simple way to accomplish this with children is to mark the dirt first with nontoxic waterbased spray paint creating the sections of where the flowers will be planted. Then, only one color of flower is brought out and planted at a time, completely finishing one color before the next planting begins. An easy guide for how far apart to plant annual flowers is to use the width of a hand between each flower in all directions.)

Plan and plant a peace garden for your community!

SHAPING YOUR WORLD

~ MATERIALS ~
- heavy paper (card stock)
- scissors
- rule
- thick glue
- paper clips
- pictures, stickers or words

Using the pattern provided, cut eight circles. Make a triangle template as shown with the dotted line. Place it on the circles and score along the edges with scissors or a pen for easy folding. Fold the flaps up. Before assembling the ball, you may place stickers, words, or pictures in the center of each triangle *. Place glue on the flaps of four circles and assemble them by using paper clips until the glue dries. This forms the top half of the sphere. Repeat the instructions for the remaining four circles which becomes the bottom half of the sphere. Glue the top and bottom halves together.

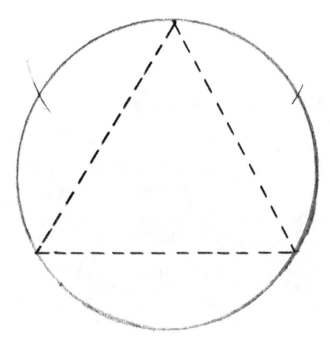

*The stickers, words or pictures placed on the ball are used to teach whatever concept you choose. For instance, questions can be made specific to renewable and non-renewable resources or animal characteristics and traits. The ball is then tossed around the circle of peacemakers. When the ball is caught, the person reads the question out loud and then answers it.

WEAVE US TOGETHER

All life on the planet is connected in an intricate life force. The slightest imperceivable change can affect entire ecosystems. Understanding the relationships of planetary life encourages the desire to share, protect, and preserve the resources rather than humankind taking what they want and robbing other life forms of what they need to survive.

~ MATERIALS ~

- yarn
- scissors
- natural fibers (jute, wool, etc.)
- found items

Buy or build a frame which will serve as your loom. Any size is fine. If this is a group project, a large (4 foot by 3 foot) stand alone frame would be nice. For individual projects, 8 inches by 10 inches would work well. The frame simply needs to be sturdy to withstand the pressure the weaving creates.

Wrap the yarn around the frame many times to create the vertical strands of the tapestry. The strands of yarn should almost touch each other along the top and bottom edges of the frame.

Go on a hike and collect feathers, twigs, long native grasses, corn stalks, etc. Weave them as well as your other natural fibers to create a tapestry. Weaving is accomplished by taking the natural fiber and threading it horizontally over and under the yarn foundation. When a few rows have been intermingled, tighten the fabric by using your fingers to apply pressure between each vertical thread to condense the horizontal fibers. To make the design more stable, it is helpful to alternate rows of natural fibers and found items with several woven rows of regular yarn. When the design is completed, the edges will be cut away from the frame, securely tying the individual fibers into groups as the tapestry is released from the frame.

SHARE as you work about how all of life on the planet is interwoven with each other. What happens when one thread (species) disappears? What are the basic living needs of all life? How can these basic needs be protected?

WATERSHED

Over two million cubic miles of fresh water lies underneath the earth's surface. This hidden resource is called groundwater. It is purified through sand, soil, and rocks, known as aquifers and is the source of drinking water and irrigation. The watertable is found at varying depths below ground and is accessed through wells which are dug, or sometimes through natural pressure bubbling up to the surface through springs. The groundwater is replenished through snow and rain which soaks into the earth. It is essential that the groundwater remain unpolluted by chemicals and other contaminants.

~ MATERIALS ~
- paper
- tape
- washable markers
- spray bottle
- water

Crumple a sheet of paper. Tape the four corners onto the second piece of paper so the crumpled sheet retains a hill-like terrain. The bottom, flat sheet represents a valley.

Use washable markers and trace how you think streams might go down the hill. Mist "the hill" generously using the spray bottle.   See how well you predicted the watershed. (The paths the water made down the hills.)

Construct another hill as before. Using the information you gathered from the first experiment, draw the pristine blue streams going down the slope. Next, using different colors of markers, add the "toxins" to the hillside land. The toxins could be litter, fertilizer, chemical spills, etc. Mist the entire hillside and notice how the toxins enter the streams, go into the valley, and eventually the groundwater supply.

SHARE YOUR THOUGHTS...

- What happens when ground water becomes polluted?
- How can you protect and preserve the ground water supply?

RHYTHM OF LIFE

The echo of a voice in a canyon, the pulse of the heart, the crash of waves breaking on the shore, the cadence of walking, the movement of the wind in the trees, even the very act of breathing all have a rhythm. The vibrations are a type of energy. The more frequent the repetition, the higher level of excitement or urgency the rhythm conveys. The reverberations of nature inspire humankind to associate meaning and connect with the larger lifeforce. Some cultures believe sound energy promotes healing; others use the beat to unite symbolically in dance, while others use it as a form of communication, or to create an environment which transcends immediate time and space. Music has been called the universal language. Whether it is used simply as a source of enjoyment or as a ritualistic shaping force, rhythm connects with something deep within the human consciousness and emancipates an ancient energy source.

~ MATERIALS ~
• drums or material to make drums

Simple drums can be made with common objects such as a piece of paper placed over the top of a cup and held taut with a rubber band.

The peacemakers will use the drums to imitate different natural rhythms. Increase and decrease the tempo (speed) and observe the difference in feeling it creates. Practice keeping a beat while you sing a song.

SHARE in a discussion about the different rhythms of life the peacemakers have noticed. Talk about how rhythm affects our mood (*e.g.*, slow breathing is calming, fast music excites).

CIRCLE OF LIFE

All living things are simultaneously consumers and producers in and of the environment. All life forms are interrelated and dependent upon each other. Harmony is a delicate balance concerning the fundamental life necessities of food, air, water, shelter, and space. Ecological peace is fostered through appreciation and respect for the oneness of the ecosystem.

~ MATERIALS ~
- copy of this page
- marker
- large piece of paper
- tape

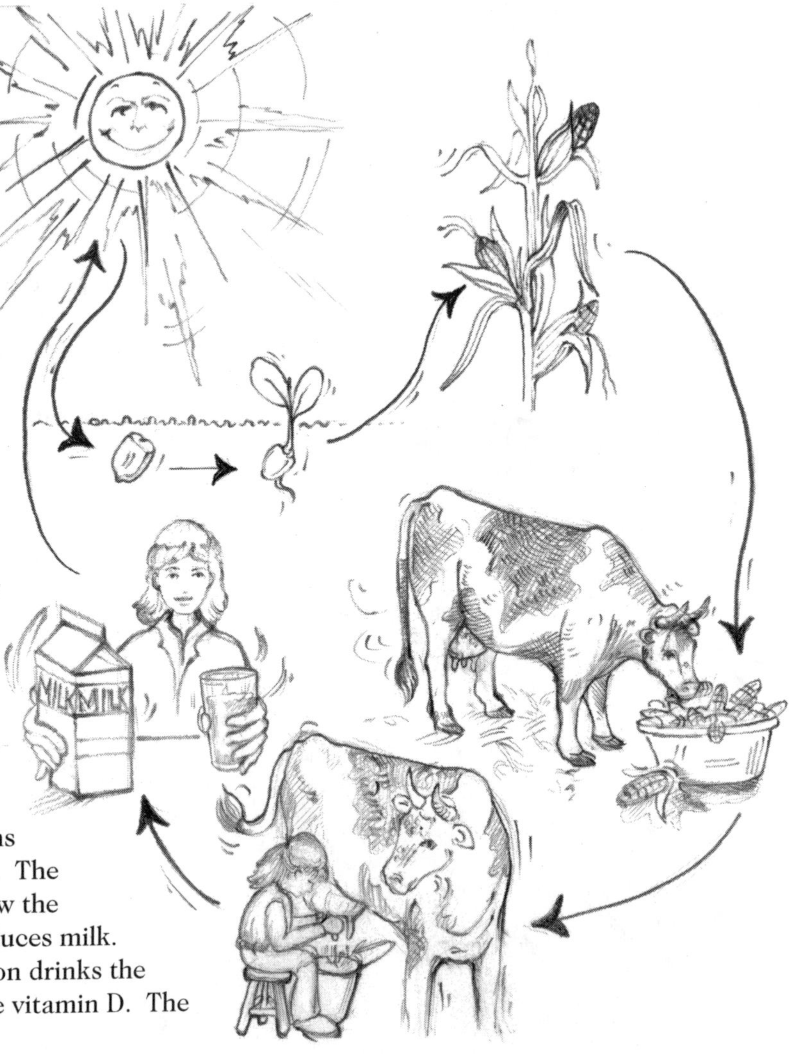

Use the tape to place the paper where everyone can see it.

Brainstorm to find the answer to the riddle "How does the sun build strong bones."

Discuss the sequence shown here. The sun warms the ground and stimulates the seed to germinate. The rain and the sun work together to sprout and grow the corn plant. The cow eats the corn. The cow produces milk. The milk is pastuerized and packaged. The person drinks the milk. The sun's rays help the body to process the vitamin D. The calcium is used to build bone tissue.

Think of other circles of interdependence and talk about them. What happens if one part of the circle is no longer available? Describe some ways different animals, insects, and plants interrelate to each other.

GET IN TOUCH

Discovery and exploration of nature facilitates a heightened sensitivity and responsibility for planetary care.

~ MATERIALS ~
- masking tape
- found natural items

Ask the peacemakers to place masking tape around one wrist with the sticky side out to create a bracelet. Make sure it is not too tight, it should be comfortable. Go on a nature walk together and collect things you find along the way. Press them onto the sticky tape until you have filled all the tape and completed your bracelet. Ideas would be flower petals, moss, feathers, leaves, small pebbles.

Another fun activity is, "Seasons of life." Pick a tree and write a description of that tree and its surroundings in each of the seasons of the year. Lay underneath the tree and draw the branches in each season.

SHARE YOUR THOUGHTS...

- Some people find a nature walk to be calming and soothing. How did it make you feel?
- Name, or imitate, sounds you heard on your walk.
- List five things you liked and two things you didn't about the walk.

ALL ELEMENTS

The "Great Hoop" is the name given to the universe by some Native American people. In his vision quest related by John G. Neihardt, Black Elk, an Oglala Sioux, saw this hoop having four sacred sections, each represented by a color. The sections designated the elements which influenced the life of his people, thunder clouds, snow, sunrise, and the sun. The color blue symbolized the power to make and destroy life; white represented healing; red, peace and wisdom; and yellow, growth. Black Elk and his people relied on the earth for their every need and held it in high regard. Respect for the earth and its forces encourages humankind to use the resources wisely, preserving and replenishing for future generations.

~ MATERIALS ~
- colored beads
- leather strip (found in craft stores)
- scissors

The peacemakers will each make a bracelet. Lengths of leather strips will vary as they need to be individually sized, but a good estimate for an ankle bracelet is 11 inches while a wrist bracelet is approximately 8 inches.

Bracelets can be made using beads to represent the universe as Black Elk envisioned it, or made like the color spectrum and rainbow – red, orange, yellow, green, blue, indigo, violet.

String the beads on the leather strip and knot as shown. The bracelet is adjusted by pulling the strips through the bead at the bottom.

SHARE in a discussion about the earth and its peoples. Name ways people show respect and disrespect for the planet.

NATURE BOOKMARKS

Conservation practices which use the earth's resources wisely, fair distribution of all resources, and appropriate disposal methods work toward peace as effective ways to protect and preserve the environment, thereby assuring the ability of the earth to sustain life for future generations.

~ MATERIALS ~

- scissors
- glue
- copies of this page
- markers or crayons
- pen
- lightweight cardboard

Give each peacemaker a copy of this page's bookmarks. They will color the bookmarks and if they want, add a quote about the joy of reading or a nice personal note to a friend. Glue the paper to the lightweight cardboard. When dry, cut out the bookmarks. Share with your friend a bookmark as well as tell them about your favorite book.

PRACTICING PEACE

The activities found in this resource are fun to do, but only make a difference as they are practiced. The development of these positive life skills benefit the individual and everyone s/he knows because they improve the quality of life.

There are many ways to implement the lessons. The commonality between all applications is that the concept is introduced, the issue is put into the context of daily life, the skill is practiced, and a time of reflection incorporates it into daily life. A few ways that have proven successful are:

PIZZA, POP, PEACE, AND MOVIE NIGHT

Once a week a family commits to practicing the skills of peacemaking. A treat of pizza and pop (soda) is shared. One or two of the activities are used as designed and full interaction occurs between the family members. Then, the family spends the rest of the night in another activity such as watching a video together. This tradition can make very sweet memories for all involved.

COMMUNITY DEVELOPMENT GRANTS

Neighborhoods join together to make a community of peace. Agencies receive the financial backing to provide trained facilitators who use the skills found within this text at community centers.

NIGHT CLASSES

School sponsored classes in peace education have been very successful in creating a new understanding. The classes are provided free to the participants and can focus on the whole family or the parenting task. This expression usually has a limited time span and is promoted through flyers and community service announcements.

PROFESSIONAL THERAPY

Some of the activities have been used very successfully by social workers and therapists as they work with individuals and groups of people with chronic needs.

PEACE FESTIVALS

A peace festival is a day set aside to celebrate peace. Hands-on activities as found in this text are common as are resource fairs where different community agencies showcase their services. A nice way to build attendance is to include performances by different multicultural groups. For more information view www.celebratingpeace.com and click on the peace festival word or icon.

LEADERSHIP TRAINING

The peace skills have proven beneficial in leadership training workshops. Whether with corporate business people or high-school leaders, the knowledge base and skills are very helpful.

CHURCH SERVICES

The activities can be incorporated into a traditional church service to illustrate an abstract concept in concrete terms so all ages can understand the lesson.

CAMPS

Many camps have incorporated the activities into their overall experience. Spending a week with a peer group focusing on peace skills is an amazing way to gain new abilities.

YOUNG PEACEMAKERS CLUBS

This grassroots global movement began in 1992 with seven children and nine adult volunteers in Sioux City, IA. Since that time, hundreds of thousands of children have been touched with the skills of peacemaking through a volunteer network – ordinary people choosing to lead extraordinary lives by making a difference in their communities.

A variety of formats of Young Peacemakers Clubs have found expression: after school groups are integrated within the curriculum, gatherings in churches and homes, and incorporated into other successful youth groups as a concentrated focus.

An in-depth explanation of Young Peacemakers Clubs are found on the following pages.

The guidelines provided in this section are not a prescription for how to have a successful Young Peacemakers Club; they are simply suggestions. The most important concept to keep in mind is your task to meet the needs of the children – empowering them with positive peacemaking skills. Don't be inhibited; do your best; your attempt is good enough!

Overall Philosophy –

The Young Peacemakers Club mission statement is "Enriching the lives of children through the pursuit of peace for all." Young Peacemakers Club is deliberately structured to provide for learning through experiencing, allowing children to explore and discover about themselves and others and to learn through discovery. Specific activities are designed to allow for divergence in skills and abilities and diversity in taste and needs. The underlying principles of Young Peacemakers Club attempt to provide a nurturing environment in which children are safe, accepted, and thereby provided opportunity to gain confidence in their ability to move into the unknown, to make choices, and to solve problems creatively.

The volunteer facilitators are challenged to suspend preconceived notions of what children need. They must be willing to let go of structure. They must live the qualities of respect for diversity, appreciation of giftedness, and celebration of life together.

The adults must be willing to develop and discover, too, about themselves and each other. An important quality of a volunteer facilitator is a genuine acceptance and love of children, not only loving children collectively, but also loving each individual child. This does not imply a passive weakness where children are allowed to be destructive to themselves and others, but an acceptance of their energy, noise, and unquenchable curiosity. Adults are encouraged to be fully present to the moment with the children, willing to join in the exuberant celebration of life and discovery.

There are no membership requirements to the Young Peacemakers Club other than presence and desire. Unlike other clubs, there is no hierarchical structure of a president, vice president, etc., but rather a sense that all are equal and all share in responsibility.

Be flexible and have fun! Adapt the material to fit the needs of the children. For instance, if the activity center requires reading capabilities the children do not possess, adjust the activity to be one where an individual reads and other children respond.

Never force a child to perform or participate in a way they are not comfortable. If they want to simply be there, honor this need.

Learning Styles and Domains –

Learning is an exciting process that continues throughout our lives. Learning occurs in many different ways for each individual. The style in which we learn best depends on our individual personality and the situation we are in when learning. Most people prefer to use one particular style or way of learning over another. Some may learn best by hearing new information, while others prefer to read new material. There are those who like to see demonstrations to grasp new concepts and still others who simply "learn by doing." Educational research has shown that the more senses we incorporate within the learning process, the more likely we are to understand, remember, and use that information again.

Field Testing –

All material has been field tested in a variety of ways to create lessons which can be understood by people of all ages. Intergenerational sharing is an incredibly valuable tool for teaching peacemaking.

Because of the belief that all people are capable of learning given the right circumstances, the material has been designed to be active and interactive for those involved. Merely reading about peacemaking or simply doing worksheets won't capture the essence of what being a peacemaker is all about, but practicing being a peacemaker certainly will.

By promoting an integration of the cognitive (thinking), affective (feeling), and psychomotor (doing) domains, the philosophy of "I am... I can... I will..." is incorporated into the lives of each young peacemaker. This viewpoint encourages the worth of each person and empowers them to make a difference in their world.

Group Participation –

Regardless of age, all are teachers and all are learners. Therefore, this material is intended to be used with groups of all ages so each can benefit from the experience and knowledge of other people. The very young are delighted to have an older child or adult work with them as a buddy. Sharing knowledge and working through a new experience is empowering at any age. There are instances, however, when specific needs demand a focus on particular issues. They enhance the learning possibilities for teens and some locations have established "Peaceable Teens Unlimited." Oftentimes this age group will focus on an issue, learn about it conceptually, and then learn experientially through a service project.

Small Relational Groups –

Two of the characteristics which shape the learning experience: People learn primarily through meaningful interaction. They learn best in a caring environment. Both of these traits are addressed through the use of small groups, which provide maximum opportunity for both meaningful interaction and in-depth caring. Many small group researchers say the ideal group is about five with the level of interaction and demonstration of caring diminishing when the group grows larger. By the time a group grows to twenty, the small group dynamics have largely disappeared altogether. Why? Consider the mechanics of interaction. In a group of five individuals, there are ten possible interactions which can be initiated between members of the group. One might expect that in a group of ten people there would be twice as many interactions, or twenty. However, a group of ten people actually has forty-five possible interactions. This means a group of ten is only twice the size of a group of five, but four and a half times as complex. What this geometric progression all means in terms of small group dynamics is simply this: The larger the group, the less likely individuals in the group will feel they know, or are known by, others in the group. There are more relationships to maintain and less time to devote to them as each new person is added to a group. And as a small group grows into large group status there will tend to be less every-member participation, more dominance by a few, and a diminished sense of satisfaction with the group.

How to avoid these losses? Form small subgroups as the larger group grows, and increase the number of activity centers were small groups can function. Provide caring group facilitators who will encourage the contribution of every person. Small groups meet one of the most basic of all human needs – to belong. Many children and adults alike in our increasingly mobile world have been cut off from the primary relationships of family and neighborhood. The impersonal nature of life in modern society has created a tremendous need for places of interaction and caring. Small peacemaking groups and Young Peacemakers Clubs are such places.

Sample Meeting Agenda –

The following is an example of what has proven effective at a weekly after-school Young Peacemakers Club group which included children ranging in ages from two to fourteen years. Adult volunteers acted as participants in and facilitators for the learning process. This particular model is high energy, uses small relation groups of about fifteen children at each center, and lasts one hour.

3:30 - 3:40 – Young peacemakers gather at the facility. New children are registered, making sure permission has been received from the parent or guardian for the child to attend the activity. The peacemakers go to an attendance chart and place stickers by their names. They then proceed to the reading chart and write in their reading times for the week.

(This individual activity of reading at home teaches tolerance through books.) Everyone finds and wears their name tags. A noncompetitive game is enjoyed by all participants. (Cooperative games are found within this text.)

3:40 - 3:45 – Children gather en masse. Any good news they want to share about their week is celebrated within the large group. (Examples include such things as buying a new puppy or, "It's my birthday!") At this time, the children also are invited to introduce any friends they have brought with them.

The peace concept of the day is then introduced. (Each week one of the four main peace themes is featured allowing for thorough coverage of the major themes.)

3:45 - 4:30 – The peacemakers divide themselves into three groups, then participate in each of the three separate activity centers (fifteen minutes at each center). The peacemakers divide into three groups to facilitate the learning and empowering possible in small relational groups. It is important to allow the children to divide themselves. If you number off or mandate who belongs in a group, you destroy the friend-to-friend bond which has already been established. To balance this, encourage the children to consciously choose not to always be with the same people from week to week.

An adult volunteer facilitator is stationed at each center and acts as the task person, simply repeating the activity as the groups of children rotate from center to center. To incorporate as many learning styles as possible, select different types of activities from this text. For instance, one center can be quiet, another involves making a craft, and the third is action oriented. Other adult volunteers rotate with the children to the various learning centers and focus on the relational aspect. This integration of task and process is extremely effective in creating an atmosphere where true learning occurs.

The meeting is closed by singing "I Want to Be a Peacemaker" and the group disbands for the day. At some point during the week, anyone new received a home visit from one of the volunteers. A very nice touch was when the volunteer arrived with a small candy bar and a note, "It's a sweet treat having you come to the Young Peacemakers Club." In this way, the volunteer was able to meet the parent(s) and develop a relationship with the family.

Code of Conduct –

The Young Peacemakers Club ought to be a safe place for all participants, a place where each person's worth and rights are valued. To help ensure this atmosphere, it is important for the peacemakers to understand that each person is accepted. However,

certain behaviors that negate the rights of others are NOT acceptable. It is helpful to establish an agreement for behavior expectations. Use the main peace sections as a catalyst for beginning the brainstorming or your code of conduct: respect for the individual, others, and property. Create a short pledge which describes the way peacemakers treat each other. Repeat this pledge often.

Name Tags –

Equality, mutuality, and a caring environment are fostered when people of all ages call each other by first name. Simple name tags made out of heavy paper with the name written on both sides can be laminated and used. This way, visitors don't feel left out or unable to talk to someone.

Teaching Peace Through Books –

Reading can help us learn about peace as we travel to faraway places and meet new people, all by turning the pages of a book. Set a personal goal of either how many pages you would like to read or how many minutes you would like to read each week. It's not important what anyone else's goal is; everyone has different interests and abilities. Concentrate on reaching the goal you have set for yourself. An excellent annotated peace bibliography can be found at www.celebratingpeace.com. Click on the book word or picture.

Marketing Your Young Peacemakers Club

Good public relations helps promote the cause of peace, gives credibility to your efforts, enhances the group's self-esteem as they become a viable presence in their community, and makes volunteer recruitment and fund-raising easier.

Decide on your audience; is your Young Peacemakers Club for all ages, or specific to a certain age? Do you want a rapidly expanding group? Or, would you prefer to stay small? When, where, and how long will you meet?

There are a wide variety of publicity methods available. Many of these alternatives require little or no cost to pursue.

The flyer is an inexpensive and effective method of communication to large numbers of people. The flyer should be printed on bright, eye-catching paper, with a clear and easy to understand message. A flyer can be distributed in any or all of the following ways: neighborhood canvassing, bulk mailing, at community events, sent through the school system, at stores where families shop.

Newspapers will publish information about your upcoming Young Peacemakers Club if you provide them with a news release. It is also helpful to make personal contact with a local reporter. The reporter may want to do a follow-up story with pictures during one of your activities or may want to use you as a source person for an interview on a related story. Also, alert the media whenever there is any special community service project going on with your club.

Public service announcements are available free of charge through radio and television stations and communicate your message to very large numbers of people.

Incentives –

The most effective way to let children and families know about Young Peacemakers Club is by personal invitation. Children are extremely good at inviting their friends to anything that they find fun. Promote this natural ability by offering incentives for attendance and for bringing a friend. Small toys, bookmarks, and other novelties work well as incentive prizes.

Fund-raising Helps –

It is recommended that no membership dues or fees be collected for the Young Peacemakers Club. Even a small fee might be cost prohibitive for some families. Sponsoring community groups or donations from local businesses are the best way to fund the workings of your club.

Additional Considerations –

Use this space to write down any additional requirements your sponsoring institution or locale may have.

SCHOOL APPLICATIONS –

The skills found in this text have been used in a great variety of ways in schools. Young Peacemakers Clubs have been used as before - and after - school programs as well as during the regular school day. Teachers have planned a class period once a week to practice the positive life skills. The abilities nurtured through this time make the regular school day go much easier as children apply what they have learned to their daily conflicts. The children have the ability to solve their own problems without the intervention of the teacher.

Another successful classroom method has been the use of a "peace table" where children can go when they have finished their assignment. Although this method is not as effective because of the lack of interaction, many skills can be worked on by the individual in this designated area. This type of assigned space has also been used as the place to go when children have conflict with one another. One of the children asks permission of the teacher and if the other child agrees, the two will go to the peace table which includes "Bridges to Understanding" and work out their differences.

An entire school decided to make the month of December their Kindness Campaign and started each day with the song being played over the loud speaker while the teachers, students, and, yes, even the principal danced to the music while singing the words.

They then placed posters all over their city. Teachers wanting to integrate the skills throughout the day will find the lessons blend nicely with multi-disciplinary programming.

Language Arts Lessons –
- Interpersonal communication skills are found on pages 72-85
- Sentence structure is found within "Silly Stories," page 38
- Sign language skills are found in "A Sign of How I Feel," page 29
- Word usage is described in "Sticks & Stones," page 85

Science Lessons –
- Centripetal force is demonstrated in "Stronger Than You Think," page 4
- Changes in matter is shown in "Time Is What It Takes," page 46 and in "Wipe the Slate Clean," page 103
- Plant chlorophyll is examined in "Make an Impression," page 56
- Molecular bonding is illustrated in "Swirling Colors," page 101
- Center of gravity is demonstrated in "Balancing Act," page 124 and in "Up Against the Wall," page 86
- Diffusion is discovered in "Wings of Kindness," page 126
- Plant life cycles are shown in "Peace Garden," page 132
- Groundwater pollutants are demonstrated in "Watershed," page 135
- Sound waves are illustrated in "Rhythm of Life," page 136
- Interconnectedness of life is discussed in "Circle of Life," page 137

Math Lessons –
- Geometry is taught in "Belonging," page 116
- Fractions and percentages are illustrated in "Mine!," page 118
- Patterns and sequences are demonstrated in "One Step Leads to Another," page 55

Social Studies Lessons –
- Native American history is explored in "Dream Catcher," page 3
- Ancient history is expressed in "Walking My Way to Peace," page 41
- Cultural symbols are found in "Peace Tree," page 104
- Cultural similarities are illustrated in "Golden Question," page 109
- Social tolerance is explored in "Just Like Me," page 112
- Cultural nuances are discovered in "Customs and Traditions," page 113
- Social injustice is discussed in "Bias," page 115
- Oppression is illustrated in "Under My Thumb," page 117

FOUR CONCEPTS OF PEACE

This puzzle may be helpful in illustrating the four concepts of peace. Notice when the pieces are placed together, a dove is formed in the middle of the puzzle. Feel free to duplicate the graphics and make T-shirts for your group of peacemakers.

May you be blessed with strength, courage, hope, compassion, and peace on your life's journey.
Enjoy your bliss!

*There came a time when the risk to remain tight in the bud was
more painful than the risk it took to blossom.*
~ Anais Nin